Craig Byrnes has seen the need for the practices of self-compassion and mindfulness in our time. The reflections and prompts he gives in this book series can certainly bring benefit to readers who follow them.

— Jack Kornfield, PhD, Founding Teacher of the Insight Meditation Society and one of the key teachers to introduce meditation to the West

With its thoughtful exercises and accessible insights, this book series offers a powerful roadmap for personal growth. Craig Byrnes has created a resource that's not only profound but also incredibly actionable. I highly recommend it to anyone seeking a deeper connection with themselves and the world around them.

— Dorie Clark is the Wall Street Journal and USA Today bestselling author of *The Long Game, Entrepreneurial You, Reinventing You and Stand Out,* which was named the #1 Leadership Book of the Year by Inc. magazine

Amazing writer. I highly recommend this book. This is not a book to read page by page in a day; take it a little at a time and savor the thoughts that go through your mind as you read these pages. The writer guides you into his world and insight. It gives you a lot to think about.

— Aaron Smith, a reader who commented on Amazon

BEGINNING

A Human's Guide
to Inner Compassion:
A 365-day Action Plan
for those who wish to
Live Life Consciously

by

Craig A. Byrnes

BEGINNING
A Human's Guide to Inner Compassion:
A 365-day action plan for those who wish to live life consciously.

Copyright © 2025 Craig A. Byrnes

ISBN 979-8-218-84061-7

You may access other books by Craig A. Byrnes at
www.ourmindfulprocess.com

Or contact Craig at:

Ourmindfulprocess@gmail.com

A NOTE TO READERS

Welcome to Our Mindful Process. We teach people why being curious from who we are, not what we think, elevates us, frees us, and empowers us! We teach mindfulness meditation, a daily practice of gently focusing on the present moment as we experience it within.

Many people think meditation is the experience of nirvana – a state of peace. That is not true. Experiencing peace during meditation does not mean we are in a place where there is no noise and pain; it's being in that noise and pain and knowing that we are having a human experience. Meditation is a daily practice of learning to pause when we are triggered and to calm ourselves as we sit with the discomfort and turmoil and breathe. It is becoming curious about the present moment. Gradually, this calming consciousness allows us to let go of anger and blame and sit with emotions that freely arise.

I believe that we learn more from our failures and our pain than we do from our successes. I have experienced a tremendous amount of pain in my life. I am a gay man who didn't want to be gay. I tried everything to change who I am, and nothing worked. In my journey toward acceptance, I've learned that when I experience pain, it awakens me, and that is an important step toward self-compassion. I have learned to look at the other side of pain. I know now that other people's opinions and discussions are none of my business.

We are so fragmented in this country because we are focusing on our dissimilarities – the 2% of what makes us different. We are all human. We all experience suffering and joy: we are all connected in this way. The world needs more compassion. This starts within.

The common definition of compassion is not the only goal of meditation. Yes, we all need kindness. But meditation brings so much more than that. When we sit quietly and we are calm and gentle with ourselves, we can see and accept what is truly happening in our lives and find peace of mind. Then we can connect meaningfully with others. Compassion is nurtured in an environment where we are all connected.

Society teaches us that knowledge is power and that solving problems is solely a thinking process. I am asking you to put those beliefs aside. I am asking you to join me in a daily meditation practice that will connect your mind with your heart. I am asking you to trust me because I have put my life back together again. I may still have my number one flaw, which is self-doubt, but when I open my heart during meditation, I come to understand what is important and how to proceed. I no longer react in anger. I am calm and I respond with compassion.

Meditation can be a spiritual experiment laboratory where we can test our ability to create new ways of acting, while watching our thinking process with new eyes. My suggestion is that you work with these four books in the series any way you like, to see where meditation and journaling take you. If your thinking mind is truly the problem, as it is for most of us, it makes no difference where you are in your life for awakening to happen.

This book series grew out of my commitment to share the benefits of meditation with as many people as I can. The goal of my organization, Our Mindful Process, is to teach people how to stop reacting to our noisy world with anger, fear, and violence by calming ourselves and opening our hearts to the creation of compassion. I see this as a path of service - commencing with ourselves.

As you begin this meditation series, there are four things to give yourself every day. The first is compassion. The world is filled with good and evil and you're not going to change that. But if you can open yourself up to another way of seeing and understanding your experience, if you can gently turn off your thinking mind, compassion will speak to you.

The next thing to give yourself is kindness. If I don't fill myself up with kindness, if I am only half full, I will ask for it back. And I won't get it back because that is not how the universe is designed. We must fill ourselves with kindness. The third element is joy. This is not the joy from money, sex, or food; it's the joy from knowing that we have shoes and food and people who love us. Many people don't have any of this. Joy comes from appreciating what we have. The last thing we need to give ourselves is balance. If I'm too kind or too compassionate, if I don't consider what I need, I may be taken advantage of. Balance is extremely important. Here are my recommendations for you as you begin.

RECOMMENDATIONS FOR THE MEDITATIVE JOURNEY

- Work on balance, not right or wrong.
- Be honest with yourself.
- Realize that it's okay not to know.
- Be gentle with yourself.
- Live in the present moment.
- Set small goals for yourself along the way.

GOAL EXAMPLES

- Physical exercises.
- Simple eating habits.
- Mental exercises.

- Emotional development exercises.
- Spiritual exercises.

HELPFUL DEFINITIONS

- Prayer – talking to God.
- Meditation – listening to God.
- Ego – that which looks out for self only.
- AM – higher self.

The time to change is now! The past is over and the future cannot be controlled. The key to action is to change our mind's awareness of the possibilities.

A VERY IMPORTANT FINAL NOTE!

This book has repetitive concepts ON PURPOSE. We learn by repetition. I'm asking that you join me in practicing meditation, reading the readings, and writing your responses each day with the intent of applying them to your life.

This book is a vehicle for experiencing an expansive consciousness that goes beyond that of the ego-driven mind. I am blessed that you even took the time to pick up the book and read this far. May you find serenity in your own journey.

January 1st

NEW YEAR'S DAY IS A holistic day to start fresh with resolutions to change our lives. This is a day to say "YES" and discover who we are underneath all we do. Rather than concentrating on changing all of our bad habits, why not come to know who we are by making a decision to turn toward the direction of the process of change?

We can begin by observing the parts of ourselves. Finding out who we are is a continuous process, not a destination. The commitment to this process takes courage. The focus changes from an exterior solution to an internal one. We will start by meditating for five minutes and add one minute each day until we reach forty minutes. Now is the moment to start practicing the benefits of meditation as a means to illuminate a larger perspective other than "me, me, and me."

Our Mindful Process

To get us started, I will share my method for meditation. I make a decision to start with five minutes a day and to increase my practice one minute each day, until the 35th day, for a total of forty minutes of meditation. In order to make a permanent change in life, we must practice a new behavior for more than thirty days. Research shows that this will increase the chance that any transformation will last long term.

For me, the only place I can depend on to actually do my meditation is on my meditation seat in my living room. I start my practice by experimenting with observing my body and senses. I begin by sitting on the outside edge of my seat with legs relaxed, back straight, and hands resting comfortably on top of my legs, upon my knees. My eyes are open, I'm gazing outward, and my mouth is slightly open. I start engaging with my meditation by taking a look at my five senses, beginning with my sense of feeling the physical body. I think about each part of my body, in order, from my head to my shoulders, and downward to my chest. I sense my stomach and then focus on where my seat meets the chair. Then I concentrate on my legs - my thighs, knees, calves - and extend my focus down to my ankles. Finally, I come to discover how my feet feel on the floor.

Once I have observed the sense of my whole physical body, making sure my posture is erect, yet relaxed and open, I start to discover my sense of sight. Lowering my head, just slightly so that my gaze is aimed at the floor, I try not to focus on any specific point. I notice my brown geometric carpet and the natural wooden flooring.

Next, I shift my attention to my sense of hearing. I choose the morning to meditate because noises are minimal. There are the sounds of the dryer in my kitchen, and the heat fan cycles on and off with the thermostat.

Next, I explore my sense of taste. It isn't so much about what I can taste. It is about focusing on how my tongue savors whatever is in my mouth at the time.

Finally, I move on to my sense of smell. The mustiness of my apartment is evident, along with the scents of food coming from my kitchen.

I expand my awareness now to focus on my breath. I breathe in and out and beyond, celebrating the movement of air in my lungs.

At this point, it isn't long before my first thoughts start to invade my solitude. I have found a precise, yet gentle, way of dealing with my mind's activity. Pema Chodron, a beloved Buddhist teacher and author, suggests that we observe our thoughts precisely, yet also very gently, and just say the word "thinking" aloud and then go back to our breath.

I have read many books about meditation that have helped me in my journey. These are my meditative notes. Now it's your turn. I encourage you to use this book or keep a journal and do the same, writing your own notes about your experiences through meditation.

How will you meditate?

1. Where is the only place you can depend on to do your daily meditation?

2. How will you time your meditations and your one-minute increments daily?

3. What journal will you keep handy to write down your thoughts?

January 2nd

LET'S GO BACK TO THE days of school. You're sitting at a desk and staring out the window, either daydreaming or being carried away by something you view outside. Without warning, you hear your name being called, along with the stern words: "PAY ATTENTION!" Remember those days?

Now that we're on the second day of our commitment to sit and get to know who we are, we can ask the question, "Just exactly what does 'paying attention' look like?"

We have all learned, at some point, how to tie our shoes. Later on, we can chew gum, have a conversation, or listen to music while we do this task. The act of tying our shoes is no longer a conscious action. To tie our shoes consciously, paying close attention to each step in the present moment, is a very different type of activity. Normal shoe tying relies on a memory of the past. When we memorize something, we move it to our subconscious.

Let's try tying our shoes consciously. First, putting our shoes on, then taking both shoelaces of one shoe in each forefinger and thumb, crossing the laces over and under, and pulling the laces to tighten them. It makes no difference whether the left lace goes over the right or vice versa. Once the laces are crossed and pulled tight, make a bunny ear with one lace. Again, it makes no difference if it's the left or the right lace. Then, make a bunny ear with the other, and hold them in each hand touching side to side. Making another choice, cross one bunny ear over the other, and then under, pushing the bunny ear into the hole and then pull. The lace is now tied. It takes total concentration to tie shoes this way - unless this is the way you have already learned.

What we're experiencing is the idea of precise attention. It's right there in the present moment – any action we do stands out when we focus on it this closely. This is meditation.

Now, with this awareness, we have the opportunity to change. Meditation allows us the leeway to add the soft and slow actions of observation, compassion, and kindness toward ourselves and toward others. These concepts may not stick right away, so we will continue practicing being compassionate and kind to ourselves without any expectation. This is the third element of meditation - the action of being open. We will come back to these three ideas over and over again.

Today is the day to add one more minute to meditation, moving to six minutes. Take a seat where you are comfortable, where it is reasonably quiet. I take a seat in my chair to explore my body and my posture. Begin to sense your physical body, from head to toe. Then move your attention to your senses of sight, hearing, taste, and smell. Today, let's think about how to be gentle and compassionate about the thoughts that may be carrying you away. Say the word, "thinking," when you are aware of your thoughts. This is a great way to be kind to ourselves. We recognize the thought is there, yet softly bring ourselves back to the present moment of our breath. To be without thoughts is not the goal.

This is a process that takes time to learn. The goal is to meditate for six minutes, with thoughts rising and falling. Then we go on with our day.

How was your experience this morning? Write your impressions and thoughts here, or in your own notebook or journal.

_____

_____

_____

_____

_____

_____

_____

_____

_____

_____

_____

_____

_____

January 3rd

WISDOM COMES TO US WHEN we slow down and become aware of each moment. Whether we call it the Holy Spirit, the wisdom mind or space, the nature of the Buddha, or quantum physics, wisdom is still the same. It is accessed by allowing ourselves to accept our thoughts and knowledge while turning our egos over to a power that is greater than ourselves. For me, that is God. For you, it may be a different spiritual source. Whatever we choose, we do so, and then we drop away from our thinking mind.

We don't control this natural force. It flows through us like the wind through the trees. We can't see it, but we come to know it. We experience it whenever and wherever we consciously practice letting go of our thinking mind.

This wisdom is neither positive nor negative; it is not part of what our culture considers universal duality. Truth is often a paradox. There is so much more to life than mere existence. Underneath all the sorrow that exists, inside every living human body, is the light of unconditional love and being. Jesus said it plainly, "The Father and I are one." Perhaps he was simply saying, "I AM." What do you believe?

I prefer to look beyond traditional religiosity. When we do that, we can sit fresh in the present moment and experience our own sense of who we really are. We aren't going to do this perfectly every moment of our lives. We can keep coming back to the present by becoming conscious of our breath.

In sitting quietly and listening to this wisdom of a higher power, there lies the energy of compassion waiting for discovery. All we have to do is be willing to ask for guidance and sit still. This is the process of accepting what is happening right now, while being open and courageous. We wait for the consciousness of wisdom to enter us in its own time.

Sitting for seven minutes is your task to commit yourself to today. Take your seat. Check your posture and explore your body from head to toe. Observe your gaze. Change your focus to hearing, then move to the taste in your mouth. Go from being curious about your sense of smell to just your breaths, in and out. The thoughts that arise during your meditation might be where you'd like to visit, or who you're thinking about. Gently, just say, "thinking," and go back to your breath.

When you finish your seven minutes, welcome the wisdom that may have come to you. Recognize that while meditating, coming back to your breath is always a compassionate gesture from your wisdom mind. Keep your commitment to meditate - to place yourself in the position to move closer to your inner wisdom.

What wisdom came up for you today?

_____

_____

_____

January 4th

In our commitment to sit and look at who we are, and what is in front of us, we are combining the physical world with the spiritual energy that gives us life. We become an experiment in quieting ourselves, so we can experience the wisdom of intuition. This process forces us to become more intimate with who we are. We are not human doings; we are human beings.

Meditation is a practice that allows us the chance to see what "not doing" can do to balance the relationship between our actions and our awareness. When we begin, we don't open to the vastness of the Universe. That focus is too broad.

In sitting meditation, we find that focusing inward and quieting the mind allows us to examine life from the inside out. This is something our thoughts may keep us from doing. Our goal is not to collect wisdom as some prize, but instead, to allow it to flow through us as we are.

Another spiritual principle comes to fruition as we sit. We are in this world, but we are not of this world. We cannot experience the spiritual realm without the ability to be physical. We are allowed to choose the option to seek the spiritual while being physical. It is not mandated; I believe it is a generous offer from the Universe.

Our physical properties need the spiritual energy that gives us life, and our spirituality needs our physical mass to make this choice. In the midst of this relationship is the balance of intuition and wisdom. We come to know the God of our understanding *is* because we *are*.

Yet the goal in meditation is not to define God. That is impossible! I believe that a spiritual power defines us over and over and over again as we come to understand, in each breath, a present-moment experience.

Today is the day for eight minutes of meditation. It's time to take your seat, become conscious of your willingness to examine your body's uprightness, and be aware of the senses of sight, hearing, taste, and smell - all bringing you to your breath. Stay aware of your posture and return to your breath.

As you sit and become aware of your mind and body, become aware of the value of your meditation process that is cultivating a new way of living. You are developing the patience to sit and just be, while continuing to come back to the breath when distracted by thoughts, by saying the word, "thinking."

While I meditate, instead of physical thinking, I try to listen for the higher voice inside me, the voice that knows. This is the voice of intuition that acts through me, expanding outward. This is higher thinking; knowing I have to turn inward for solutions.

Today is a practice of letting go. I am letting go of my need to control events or people, and letting God handle them. What does that look like for you? Some people write down their worries and put them in a box so they can practice patience, not perfection. Today is a day to recognize progress, not perfection. Perfection is a spiritual disease; one where the goal is to control an outcome. Outcomes are in the future. Here we focus on the present moment. Coming back to your breath will help you stay in this moment. Set aside the past and the future. Breathe and become aware of your inner feelings. Practice letting go of other voices inside your mind and out in the world.

_____

_____

_____

_____

_____

_____

_____

_____

_____

_____

_____

_____

January 5th

IN OUR SEARCH INWARD, WE can come to see that what we do, how old we are, and what we feel, change from moment to moment. What doesn't change is who we are. The force that gives us life is constant and the ultimate in consciousness.

By starting with who we are, we become grounded and connected to that which gives everything life. Let's not get all bogged down in religiosity; let's not try to pigeonhole this force. Instead, let's start by making a decision to give more space to our narrowed experience. Let's make space for tender loving-kindness. Moving away from the idea of receiving some sort of reward for our actions, let's hone in on the sensation of compassion that is called tender loving-kindness. This comes from within, from the space of who we are.

As you take a deep breath in, take in all of the stressful sensations that you're encountering right now. Focus on each of your senses as you breathe slowly and evenly. Now become aware of whatever emotion arises, and breathe out tender loving-kindness for yourself.

The more space we give to each moment as we sit, the greater our ability to sense tender loving-kindness. If you don't yet know what this sensation feels like, just focus on giving more space to your practice. We don't force tender loving-kindness; it comes to us when we are aware of our own tender feelings such as sadness or grief.

It comes to us when we offer our vulnerability in our meditation practice. The experience of tender loving-kindness comes to flow naturally, from who we are, in its own time.

Today is the day for nine minutes of meditation. Bring your physical self to your seat, explore your posture clearly while gently moving through your other senses of sight, sound, taste, and smell. If today brings you a whirlwind of thoughts, see each of them clearly, and then let them go by saying, "thinking." Doing this opens you to the idea and experience of tender loving-kindness.

It is sometimes challenging to let go of these thoughts gently. Sometimes we feel strong feelings and we are not very kind to ourselves. Yet, just practicing letting go of troubling thoughts while sitting with the emotions of fear, anger, shame, or sadness is enough for today. Even the thought, "I am not kind to myself," becomes something I treat like a meditation thought – I say "thinking" and I let it go. Letting go is practicing tender loving-kindness toward myself. This new behavior is not smooth, and it doesn't have to be. I have to remind myself this is a process, not a destination.

Remember that the daily noise that occurs in your mind during meditation is not a permanent predicament. Later in the day, these thoughts and your feelings about them may just dissolve if you let them go. What I think about never stays the same. Only who I am remains constant. This is a new idea to embrace. I have to continue my meditation practice, with the hope that this process will stick.

What are some kind words you can say to yourself?

January 6th

THE WORLD NEEDS MORE COMPASSION. It starts within. It is nurtured in an environment where we are all connected. The common definition of compassion is not the goal. The goal is to see what is.

In order to heal our lives, this focus inward brings us to a place of great sadness. We all have lost someone dear to us or have experienced big disappointments in life. Having compassion for ourselves begins with going to the space created by meditation; this act starts the healing in our lives.

We can begin the grieving process suggested to us by Elizabeth Kubler Ross. She shows us how to explore the five stages of grief:

- Denial that we have a problem.
- Anger that comes from facing the truth of what is.
- Bargaining and procrastination that steer our focus away from taking personal responsibility for our feelings.
- Sadness.
- Acceptance that allows us to practice compassion.

Being empathetic with ourselves helps us to open our hearts in three distinctive ways. First, we become the individuals who are in the process of awakening in the midst of those feelings, letting go of those thoughts. We expand our consciousness, which brings us to compassion. Second, we start to expose ourselves to the spiritual teachings of cosmic law - limitless principles of pure truth and wisdom. And third, we seek out connection to others on the path of spiritual growth.

Here we begin to become curious about being conscious of the present moment and how this consciousness allows us to let go of blame and sit with emotions that freely arise. We are committed to the path of educating ourselves to open our hearts to the creation of compassion. We introduce our commitment to the path of service - commencing with ourselves.

Today is the day of ten minutes of meditation. Taking your seat, begin your pledge to start each new day fresh. Without judgment of your thoughts as they come, just by saying "thinking" and letting go of each thought, you will begin to see how most of your thoughts are about reliving the past or trying to figure out what is going to happen in the future. By gently stopping those thoughts and returning to your breath, you can experience what is happening right now.

In this moment, I can see the root of my urge to fix the past or control the future. Sometimes I feel anger or regret about what I have done – or haven't done. What about you? Stay in the now of your breath and allow yourself to feel any feelings you are aware of that are rising inside you.

_____

_____

_____

January 7th

BRINGING NATURAL PEACE AND JOY into our lives takes willingness. Creating a space for that peace is a decision based on choice. When we choose to meditate, we learn to accept what happens in our life, moment by moment. If we let go of trying to control the Universe with what we believe is right, we can experience a path to comfort and familiarity with our intuition, the undefined source of power that comes from life itself.

Whatever we're feeling or thinking, we just recognize and acknowledge what is there, without the need to change a thing. Going inside and focusing on our breath, taking in all that is, we come to the present moment where all peace and joy flow. Relying on compassion and kindness, we can open ourselves to the process that has no beginning or end.

Today's meditation is for eleven minutes. Sit comfortably and become aware of your physical body and your senses, one by one. You know how to do this now, so hopefully the process is becoming a little easier, day by day! One of the great benefits of meditation is that you can stop and restart your day whenever you need to. In this way, you are allowing yourself to touch the loving-kindness within you and to feel peace and joy flow from the expanse of your breaths. When you are finished, write down what you experienced while meditating today.

_____

_____

_____

_____

_____

_____

_____

_____

_____

_____

_____

_____

_____

January 8th

WE ARE BORN TO OUR first breath. There will never be an inhaled breath without an exhalation. In meditation, we become aware of this balance of opposites. We always return from whence we came. The spiritual term for balance is equanimity.

As we practice today, let's feel the cycle of breathing akin to the movement of the tide's ebb and flow. Then, if we start thinking, wandering away from our awareness of the breath, we can accept the contemplation and come back to the center of balance. We focus our awareness again on the breath.

Meditation takes us out of our heads and into our hearts - the core, the center of our being. Here there is no blame, only the flowing of emotions and the sensations they create on our visceral journey inward.

Today we will meditate for twelve minutes. The focus today is on balance. We will watch our thoughts and give them the space that our breath provides, so that balance can be maintained naturally.

How was your practice today? Write down your thoughts and reactions here or in your journal.

January 9th

ONLY WE KNOW WHERE OUR mind is today. We can either be in full drive with our obsessive thoughts, aggressive urges, yearning for something or someone, or we can be totally nonchalant, or simply remain dull inside our thought processes.

Wherever we are, we have the opportunity, on the meditation chair or cushion, to *know* where we are. We are the only ones who can recognize how our mind is doing today. No one can do that for us.

Once we have identified where we are, we can use that point to move toward the center of our being. This is working with the process of steadying the mind. We begin to work with our compulsive thoughts about what is happening outside of our control. We identify what dissatisfies us and gently become present to identify what inside us is out of balance.

Being present allows us to become empowered. Our own personal power is not achieved by allowing our ego to be in control. We can begin to feel our inner strength as we learn how to see, hear, smell, taste, sense, or think without being carried away by discursive thoughts driven by the past or the future.

Today we meditate for thirteen minutes. Find your seat and become aware of your body and your senses, one by one.

Today's focus is on how to compose yourself, no matter how your meditation starts, and no matter how your day goes. It doesn't matter how you feel today. There need be no critique. All you need to do is practice being more conscious of your breaths than you were before you began this session. See where you are, accept where you are, and allow the Universe to do the rest. Your breath is your safeguard that allows you to rest in your soul, your inner being. This is how you steady yourself.

What can you accept about yourself today?

_____

_____

_____

_____

_____

_____

_____

_____

_____

January 10th

IN BEING WITH THE BREATH, the object of our abiding, of our presence, is sensing the air flowing inward and outward. Scrutinizing the breath is not the goal. To do so moves us toward the idea of "thinking" about the breath. The idea is just to be with the breath, not to identify with it.

We meditate with our eyes open. The idea is to integrate our meditative practice with what is actually going on in the world around us. To shut our eyes is to compartmentalize our meditation into some sort of ideal. This separates us from the world.

Perhaps we can begin to discover some small "aha" moments, either in our practice or when we finish. Every single session is different. Sometimes I become aware of positive emotions, sometimes negative ones. Sometimes I feel shame about what I have done in the past. Shame goes beyond guilt. Shame is feeling bad for *who I am* not *what I have done*. Shame comes from being judged harshly, perhaps when young.

It's not whether our meditation practice is good or bad, fluid or stuck, but whether we are observing our thoughts, feelings, and sensations, along with sights, sounds, and smells all around us.

Today we meditate for fourteen minutes. We start with where you are in the present moment. Whatever you have done in the past is in the past. Coming back to the breath, being in the now, means being gentle with yourself, without blaming inward or outward.

What are you noticing today? What are the sensations, sights, sounds, and smells around you? This is how we stay in the present moment.

_____

_____

_____

_____

_____

_____

_____

_____

_____

_____

_____

_____

January 11ᵗʰ

WHILE JOURNEYING THROUGH OUR PRACTICE of meditation, we experience "clear-seeing," a new clarity of being. We can add to our clear-seeing the characteristics of gentleness and relaxation. Too much tightness in our concentration can actually increase our discursive thoughts. Too loose a concentration and our practice becomes dull.

Expanding on clear-seeing, we can add gentleness to balance our routine.

1. Gently experience the inward breath.

2. Gently explore the body and feeling states.

3. Gently become aware of discursive thought, labeling it "thinking."

4. Gently exhale, letting go and letting God.

There is a genre of meditation called Tonglen, a Buddhist practice of taking in others' pain and sending them compassion. It is not the ultimate, correct way to practice. Right and wrong judgment is not the goal here. Adding friendliness to whatever format we're using allows us to connect to who we are. The path is the goal, not the destination, of peaceful existence. Perfection is never achieved, yet our balance between clear-seeing and gentleness may bring us to less suffering than an ego-driven life might. The powerful force that changes our lives only exists "NOW." The present moment brings us to the possibility of wisdom. We let go of the idea of what's in it for our ego.

By exploring inwardly, we are performing an act that is called: cleaning *only* our side of the street! Through this practice, we are inventorying ourselves. We are taking a close look at our actions and, by gently discovering our good and bad points, we find a middle path that rises above an understanding of the physical realm.

We have now reached fifteen minutes of meditation. Adding gentleness to our daily life, we make a decision to clearly see our strongest character defects. One of mine is not asking for help. When I think about asking someone to help me with something, my thoughts go to the future, to the reaction that person might have to my asking for help. He or she might think I am weak for asking, or they might criticize me for not knowing how to do this on my own. This is my over-active mind jumping ahead with fear and anxiety. Coming gently back to the present moment, I come to believe in the courageousness of my action. It does take courage to ask for help. The outcome is not in the present moment. Gently coming back to my breath, I exhale. Focusing on my inward and outward breaths, I warmly let go of my fear and, staying with the process of meditating, I stay in the spaciousness of simply being.

What can you ask for help with today?

_____

_____

January 12ᵗʰ

WHETHER WE'RE AT AN OFFICE or wandering around in a fog of rumination on the street, we can all treat our meditation practice like freshly baked bread! There's a spaciousness to experiencing the smell of bread right out of the oven. The opposite would be treating our practice like a stale product. Knowledge is not the focus, as that's not fresh. Thinking is often about the past or the future. The present moment is the bread of our practice, coming right out of the oven, all fresh and calling for the kind of attention that brings us peaceful joy. This is the path to wisdom, which does not need thought.

A fresh curious approach, neither judgmental, craving, nor unconscious, allows us to be open to the central place within, that brings us insight. We don't make it a goal to completely disregard our bodies, trying to reach some sort of nirvana. Instead, we bring our internal selves to our practice, while being a "watcher" who observes and connects us to what we do. By reading this book, we learn what moves us from the center of serenity. We are not striving toward goodness or away from bad. We are moving toward a quiet place where we can find relief.

We do this by continuing to return to the breath, over and over. In little bits and pieces, we gain the understanding of how letting go of our ego's desire to control outcomes allows our Higher Inner Self

to bring us to the sanity of serenity. Letting go and letting God is about leaving room for the Universe to speak to us about its wisdom.

Today we meditate for sixteen minutes. Let's focus on the choices we have when we take the time to meditate. Letting go of what I want or think I need, allowing the space of silence to appear in the midst of all my thinking, allows me to become more comfortable with the uncertainty of day-to-day life. Do I still think my way into dissatisfaction? Sure I do! Am I making progress with creating a new path? Absolutely! I just have to stop and smell the bread coming out of the oven.

Practice returning to your breath every time a thought enters your mind. Does this help you relax your mind and heart?

_____

_____

_____

_____

_____

_____

_____

_____

January 13th

PAIN IS A PART OF our physical existence. Most of us, through compulsive thought, focus on the negative aspects of life, not the positive. There lies the problem. We don't have a larger understanding of pain. We have to surrender to a larger perspective. We evolve through pain when we become conscious of its greater purpose.

Insanity is doing the same thing, over and over, expecting a different result. The question I can ask myself is: "Why am I dissatisfied?" Then, I bring that question into my practice. With patience, the answer comes to me. My ego's view is limited. Everyone feels pain! It's not just me. We all share this in common. Pain connects all of us!

The solution, in our meditative practice, is to invite the pain in without fueling it with our ruminations. We make it our practice, by saying, "thinking," to focus instead on the rawness of what we perceive as negative emotion. Once we truly own the energy of emotion, our inner awareness can shower us with compassion and tender loving-kindness. Once we experience the healing, we can extend that to others who are in the same boat.

Today we meditate for seventeen minutes. Let's examine pain and suffering from a spiritual point of view, using our physical ability to act and to move to a higher level of understanding.

My inner self alone can't act. It needs the physical me. Yet, I'm imperfect. I need to accept that, too. I need my internal spiritual self to achieve progressive wisdom.

I'm dissatisfied when my focus is on the physical alone because I spend the majority of my day in my mind, in discursive thought, not in my body. Is this inherently wrong, or sinful? I go back to the root of the word "sin". Think of sine and cosine in geometry. These mathematical references are from the point of rest, or zero. I'm of the understanding that sine /sin is the movement away from balance. I'm aware that it is compulsive thinking that tears me away from the focus of the present moment. The physical me experiences duality, both positive and negative. Both of these aspects pull me in either direction, causing an imbalance. Therefore, I miss the mark.

We only need our imperfect physical selves to act in the present moment, gently turning away from "thinking". Transformation becomes possible through this path. I come to hit the mark above the realm of time and space. This takes courage and faith.

With a spiritual outlook, I can live in the physical world while holding my balance with the understanding and wisdom that we all suffer. I'm not alone. Through my active meditative practice, I can focus on the spiritual center of just "being". Through love, I am able to go back to the garden of eternal life.

What is your place of peace?

_____

_____

January 14th

ANCHORING OUR CONSCIOUSNESS IN THE present moment can be advanced by continuing to add all the senses of our human existence. Exploring sight, sound, smell, taste, and the sense of physical feeling further enhances our rooting in the "NOW". Once we add a particular sense to our practice, we may later alternate and combine these perceptions with the breath.

Let us begin with the sense of sight. When we have started our session, checking our posture and being with our breath, we launch our opportunity to be with color, texture, and brightness. There is no evaluation, only the realization of what we see. Our gaze may be short or long, high or low. If we start to contemplate what we are viewing, we can gently stop by saying the word, "thinking", and secure ourselves again.

Today we meditate for eighteen minutes. Look out your window. What do you see? Today I see the mountains, along with a patchwork of gray trees that look like upward sticks, and a mosaic of evergreens that extend for miles. The only movement is the clouds as they dance over the highlands, casting their shadows over the grayness of the trees.

The blue sky is at one with the clouds. The sun appears in and out of the clouds, moving forward and back to embrace the mountains as it continues to set. My first sight of the setting sun is yellow, then it turns orange, and finally the sun turns to red as it slides behind the ridge.

The blue sky becomes yellow at sunset above the skyline. The clouds take on a pink and gray hue. I make the decision to continue my practice, to be with the process of describing what I am seeing. The atmosphere expresses its twilight. The clouds become a muddy patchwork over the stubble of trees on the mountains. Darker and darker the colors become; the dimming summit swallows the trees until there is no detail. I go back to my breath.

Describe the sky that you see from where you are. Is it sunny or cloudy, bright or dark? Are the stars out tonight?

_____

_____

_____

_____

_____

_____

_____

_____

_____

January 15th

AS THE ANCIENT PHILOSOPHER ARISTOTLE said, "Nature abhors a vacuum." This means that something always slips into an empty space. The idea of adding the consciousness of our senses to the practice is not to eliminate thought altogether. That's impossible. Including the senses purely moves us to the path of stabilizing our minds.

Sound is natural and abundant daily in a busy life. Ironically, it's as prevalent as discursive thought is in our heads. In our practice, we season our consciousness with the friendly acknowledgement of the noises around us as we move away from evaluating what we hear. We focus instead on another part of our inner selves.

This is the process of coming to know a life above our thoughts. We learn to give up control, developing the willingness to sit quietly and observe, as a life skill. Just as we come to discover thought, we approach what we hear by being present for it, without judgment. Being with the sound of silence – or near silence - connects us with the space of being.

Today we meditate for nineteen minutes. I choose the library to work with sound. This is not a silent place; however, it has less volume than most places.

Of course, my attention to the breath is distracted, not only by my thinking, but also by the low rumbling conversations at the many tables here. It isn't long before I become attentive to the thought, "*I am easily drawn away by voices, my own or others. I am aware of how I put excessive value on what other people say!*" These are thoughts, so I silently say, "thinking." I continue to train my mind by listening to the voices without being lured away by my judgment.

Underneath the conversations are a host of other sounds to behold:

- The turning of pages.
- The squeaking or movement of chairs and tables.
- The clicks and hums of the copy machine.
- A singular cough.
- The sound of footsteps in all directions.
- Doors opening and closing.
- The sound of the mechanics of a stapler.
- The sliding of a book from and back to its shelf.
- The dropping of various objects on tables.

I become aware that it's not the sounds that are the issue. It is what my mind does with these sounds. It starts creating a story about them. So I come back to the act of listening. Just noticing which sounds are closer and which are further away, strengthens my sense of wellbeing. It is another way of experiencing a connection to the present moment.

I move to a vacant seat in a quiet study room to continue my practice for a few more minutes and to hear what I can perceive. With the sound of the closing door, I can hear my heartbeat. This brings me right to my breath. My heartbeat and my breath are always there. I'm here to listen to both and settle in. I realize I was too distracted by all the other noises in the open library space, leaving no room for me to be aware of my breath. So I stay here to continue my meditation in relative peace.

Spend some time in your public library today. What do you hear? Can you concentrate where there is sound, even if it is relatively quiet?

_____

_____

_____

_____

_____

_____

_____

_____

_____

_____

_____

_____

January 16th

TODAY, OUR MEDITATION TIME EXPANDS to twenty minutes. Let's explore expanding our meditative practice by adding the sense of smell. We're not attempting to give any value to particular odors or scents. Judgmental words won't help us to experience a smell. We simply invite whatever smell meets us into the present moment. If our bodies react, we notice that, as well, and continue to go back to the act of smelling. If we get carried away, "thinking" about any particular item we've smelled, we can recognize that and come back gently to the act of smelling in general.

Different places have either an abundance or a limited set of scent offerings. Our own living spaces contain a plethora of smells. It's not about where we choose to go; it's about preparing an open mind in the midst of our choices, wherever we happen to be.

Let's try a walking meditation today, instead of sitting on a bed or chair. Notice your breath while walking slowly. Replace your focus on the sounds of your footsteps with whatever enters your sense of smell.

This morning, I walk by a bakery. I stop as I notice the scent of baking bread. Walking inside the bakery to experience a stronger scent, I take a moment to breathe in the aromas of yeast, bread, and pastries baking in the ovens. Both the dough and I are in meditation together. We are both rising with the breath.

Where can you walk for meditation today?

_____

_____

_____

_____

_____

_____

_____

_____

_____

_____

_____

_____

_____

January 17th

TODAY WE WILL BRING THE sense of taste into our practice. We will become aware that when we eat, our mind is usually racing. We're also not at the point of nirvana where we can be one with every single moment of taste. With that in mind, we'll have to take the middle road and practice by repeatedly returning to our sense of taste.

We don't have to go to the library to study the tongue, we can simply experiment with what we put in our mouths. The tongue has specific receptors where we are conscious of sweet, sour, bitter, and salty tastes. The key is to be curious and explore each experience.

If we get distracted by giving any value to a specific taste, such as, "This is too salty", we must return to the act of tasting, itself, and gently let go of the thought by labeling it, "thinking".

Today we meditate for twenty-one minutes, focusing on our sense of taste. I take my seat on my meditation chair, set my posture, turn inside to notice my breath, and slowly add sips and spoonfuls of different foods. I have selected several foods that I love, which is a way showing self-compassion.

A sip of peppermint tea and honey helps me to explore where I taste sweetness and spice. My sense of smell really adds to the experience, as the peppermint vapor fills my nose. I find it difficult to separate the two senses while tasting the peppermint on my tongue. But I notice that if I concentrate on my breath and the taste of peppermint, the scent anchors me into the present moment. Practicing three levels of consciousness at once makes it difficult to have a thought! This is working for me. Next, I notice that the sweetness of the honey makes the peppermint smoother. This is a thought, though, and I'm just here to be with the honey and the tea.

I have also selected peanut butter to taste. I put a spoon in the peanut butter and slide it into my mouth. My tongue spreads it out and the taste of peppermint and honey are muted by its thickness and earthiness. The peanut butter is colder on my tongue than the tea. That's a feeling sensation. Wow, a fourth dimension of consciousness to behold! Peanut butter is sweet and nutty. It's smooth.

I take a sip of tea and the heat of the liquid strips my tongue, allowing me to cleanse my palette and swallow. I take another sip to savor the sting of the spice with the nectar of the honey syrup. The closer I get to the bottom of the mug, the sweeter the mixture becomes. Honey is slow to dissolve, even in hot tea. That's a thought, so I go back to savoring the experience by tasting another spoonful of peanut butter.

What tastes can you savor today?

_____

_____

_____

_____

January 18th

OUR NEXT LEVEL OF CONSCIOUSNESS is the state of physical sensation. We are continuing to strengthen our practice. But first, go back to January 1st and review the six points of reference to our bodies. Then, begin by taking a seat, legs relaxed, adjusting your posture, placing your hands on your knees, bringing your gaze to the front with eyes open while allowing your mouth to stay slightly open, to let the air flow.

There is so much you can notice by being with your body. Face forward as you begin. Start at the top of your head and name and notice each body part as you go down to your toes. Or, bring your awareness to your feet and toes and go up. The focus is *not* where you start. It is just becoming aware of the different parts of your body. You're not judging how your body feels. Just be conscious of each body part, as you move up and down.

Today we meditate for twenty-two minutes, focusing on a progressive awareness of each of the parts of our bodies. I observe the six points of my physical body when taking my seat. I am in touch with my breath. Once I am at a point where I say "thinking" to any mind chatter, and my mind becomes stable, I start at the top of my head. The point is to range over my body, sensing the energy of what it feels like in that area. Let's do this together. Focus on each part, while noticing your breath:

- top of your head
- your ears
- your eyes
- your nose
- your mouth and tongue
- your throat (swallow)
- your chest (rising and falling with each breath)
- your shoulders
- down your arms to each hand and each finger (the sensation of your hands on your knees)
- back up your arms and down to your gut
- where you gut meets your seat
- your seat upon the chair
- your thighs against the chair frame
- your knees (the sensation of your knees supporting your hands)
- down each leg to your feet
- the feeling of your feet on the floor, then your toes individually

Now, back up.

I let go of any thoughts or conversation I may desire to have as to what I am sensing in my body. This process isn't simple or difficult. It just is.

What are you noticing in your body as you practice this method of meditation?

January 19th

MEDITATION ALLOWS US TO OBSERVE our senses and our surroundings, and then gently make a decision to train our minds so that we can pause before reacting to negative experiences or emotions. Everyone feels pain. Suffering is a part of life. Facing pain while letting go of the thoughts that fuel it, creates calm, a new wisdom, and a softer path. We come to know the concept of impermanence. Things are constantly changing. There is the birth of any given situation, followed by its death as it is replaced by the next event of the moment.

Concentrating on the breath allows us a 360^0 view of life and death. We are in a place of observation. Coaching our minds from this new perspective allows us to rise above the worlds of good and evil, the world of duality. We come to the place where we can say, "This too shall pass." From this place, we can add compassion to what we clearly see, opening up our hearts to receive from the Universe what we need to simply be in the present moment. We begin to develop intuition about our patterns of thought in reaction to the emotions we feel.

We will practice twenty-three minutes of meditation today. Today I'm aware that my mind is filled with thoughts of the past. I do my very best to come back to the breath; however, my mind is totally preoccupied. Does this happen to you? Of course, it does. We are human. Meditation teaches us not to judge these thoughts, only to observe them. I can see two distinct issues of thought feeding my churning emotions.

The first issue is a lack of compassion I sometimes have for myself. I can now understand how going over any past situation obsessively is not kind, nor is it helpful in any way. In coming back to my breath, I am relinquishing my power over this thought. Just let it go, with a breath. Breathing calmly while saying, "Let it go, Craig," creates space in my mind. And in this space, there is room for a power greater than myself to relieve me and to heal me of my obsessive and compulsive thoughts about the past and about the future. When I am absorbed in thinking about the past, I am focused on the things I've done that I regret, or the things other people have done that upset me. When I'm focused on the future, I might be worried or fearful about something that might happen. Either way, I am not able to be present for the current moment. Consequently, when I am in this state of distraction, with worry, fear, sadness, or anger, I lose things. I'm so preoccupied with what is going on in my head that I totally lose mindfulness of what is going on around me. Where did I put my keys? Where is my wallet?

Once I realize I have lost something, I obsess about the outcome of my search for that which was lost. And as I am sitting with this dilemma, I do not wish to push it away. I must find my lost things! But my experience shows that I will not find them in this state of agitation. I need to calm my mind and simply accept that I have lost these items. I practice the mind-training slogan to be compassionate and kind to myself. This is a new way of looking at myself and this situation.

Today is the day to practice being present so that I can deal more effectively with losing something. The key, for me, is to accept what is, while adding a small space, through my conscious breathing, for the necessary self-compassion to make better choices, whatever they may be.

Obsessing about trying to remember where I left something, berating myself for losing it, trying anxiously to control the outcome of finding it, are all thoughts in the past or the future. What comes to mind, in creating a pause by taking a deep breath, is a Buddhist saying, "Drive all blame into one." This is pointing out how to use blame effectively, which is to see ego-clinging to the problem. This expression comes from the 59 Slogans of Lojong. These are 59 sayings that help the individual expand consciousness from the viewpoint of the ego. Feel free to search Wikipedia for the word Lojong.

Today, I comprehend that when I lose material things, I have allowed my inner fears to be fed by revisiting the past or trying to control the outcomes of the future.

Let's be grateful for our breath. We are training our minds by associating our breath with new and peaceful ways of being, rather than reacting to painful events. We are making progress in the process of change. We are on the path of healing. I agree to let go and let God, my higher power, guide me.

What is your inner wisdom telling you?

_____

_____

_____

_____

_____

January 20th

LET'S EXPLORE THE PHRASE, "LET go and let God." Instead of conjuring up old thoughts and beliefs about the "G" word, we can start fresh in the present moment and make the choice to create a new, expanded outlook.

When we become aware of our bodies, we can see how letting go of our emotions, once we are aware of them, relaxes us. When we add tender loving-kindnes to our practice, our physical relationship to the world becomes more serene. As we increase our cognizance of each part of our anatomy, we spend less time in the compulsive thoughts that feed our conflicting emotions. We gradually learn to let go of our worries with the understanding of what we can and cannot change, and then changing what we can through our concentration. We don't deny the emotion behind our worries, we change our perspective to just be with what troubles us, and let God handle it.

We can now face the continuous chatter in our minds with an increased awareness and scope of inner peace, which we can visualize as a vastness and emptiness. Letting go of any thought, without labeling it good or bad, allows us to start any moment over, at any time. We can change any direction we're headed, such as storing up resentments, and drop the pebbles of discontent before they grow into boulders around our necks.

We can become more conscious of any feelings we have by owning what I call our FLAGSS (fear, loneliness, anger, guilt, shame, and sadness) and letting go from the space we develop in our hearts. By doing so, we become more honest about owning our emotions 100%, while starting to replace the stress of control with the peace of compassion toward ourselves.

What we release is our ego's need to master an outcome. What we need to fill the void is our trust in a renewed faith and hope. We remain in the world, but we focus our vision on the realm of spiritual eternity. We come to know that everything physical has a beginning and an end. The spiritual act of meditation is ethereal; it brings up pure love. We are fulfilled from the inside, becoming a living conduit of being-ness that knows no end.

God is not externally defined, but experientially confirmed. You can choose your own higher power. Letting go is an action by which we can increase our familiarity with, and daily experience of, peace. We are not in charge of everything, and we can't make things happen, or prevent them from happening. We open ourselves to experience the relief by trusting God or a higher power to help us.

Today we meditate for twenty-four minutes. Let's focus on one of the most difficult emotions in the human experience - one that gets us in the most trouble - anger.

We all get angry. It is what we do with that anger that either gets us into trouble or gets us gradually into a state of calm. Here are the steps that will help you respond constructively to situations that cause anger:

- Have a direct experience with the anger. Feel where it resides in your body. Now send a breath there. Breathe in and out to calm that spot.

- Move away from identifying with the duality of who is right and who is wrong. Do not focus on blame, and do not give your power away to another.

- The goal is to use your awareness to take the best action. Often this is taking the high road in a way that brings peace. It could mean apologizing for your part in the situation. This opens the door for a calmer conversation.

Anger is our most challenging emotion. Often, we revisit things that made us angry, and we can get upset all over again while judging what happened. This is the ego, the thinking mind at work. When this happens, we can realize what is happening and move from the past to the present moment. Understand that revisiting a past resentment is only going to ruin *yourself* - not the other person. Again, let go and let God or your own higher power take care of it! We now know how to be open and spacious enough to be fully present with the moment in front of us.

What is one resentment you can ask to be relieved of? Write it down and let God or your higher power lift it from your mind.

_____

_____

_____

_____

_____

January 21ˢᵗ

THE INTENTION OF MEDITATION IS to spend time in silence to create the space necessary to be open to wisdom within the spirit and to turn away from knowledge within the mind. This wisdom is not predictable, nor can we crave it or control it into existence. We must become willing, in our practice, to be available to receive it.

We move in a direction that makes progress, not perfection. Just a gap of quiet mind allows us to deepen our relationship with this space, to gently become aware of our tendency to blame either ourselves or what's in front of us, as the culprit for our unhappiness. This momentary pause, taken over and over by saying "thinking", helps us clean our side of the street with a double-edged sword. Clear- seeing and the practice of compassion starts within us, first. This place in the middle cuts to the heart of the matter We fuel our practice by being willing to take a step toward creating steadfastness.

Today's meditation will be twenty-five minutes long, and we will focus on the fear that comes with self-doubt. For me, the solution is simple. There is no self to fortify in silence. There is only the energy of fear to place at the altar of wisdom. Underneath any self-righteousness is this fear. Between the inward breath and the outward breath, I come to be available for wisdom to speak to me. This wisdom is random. I cannot pin it down. I cannot think it into existence. I use the three Cs to detach from painful events: I can't control them, I don't cause them, and I can't cure myself of the dissatisfaction that comes with powerful, painful emotions.

Yet in meditation, I can yield to the force greater than what my ego believes. I want a solution to all my problems. I want to be free from fear and self-doubt. These thoughts have two errors: the emphasis on "I" and the craving of "want".

Let's meditate today with an intention. Let's intend to be willing to sit today. It's that simple. The power of wisdom does the rest. We come to believe in a power greater than ourselves that restores us to sanity. This is the second step of any 12-step recovery program. Sanity is always available. It's not lost. I just become aware of it. I am planting the seeds of compassion and kindness – toward myself and others.

My intention is to be able to sit with painful emotions and recognize when I am out of balance. I know that everything is impermanent, except for who I am.

What is your intention in your meditation today?

_____

_____

_____

_____

_____

_____

January 22nd

AS WE CONTINUE TO SEE our lives as clearly as we can, and compassion bring us toward a peaceful center, we set the stage for how we deal with speech. Speech is the language and the messages that come from others, and even more importantly, that which comes from within us.

Language can be bitter. Adding our own bitter speech to a conversation or situation further poisons the total experience. It indicates a life that is off-center. Staying away from judgment, we raise our level of consciousness around our use of speech. This is a huge undertaking. We can wisely admit that we will have failures in achieving the goal of uplifting speech. The solution is better reached if we see ourselves as connected to the whole. Speech affects everyone.

There's a verse to a song that comes to mind, bringing focus to the target of speech:

"Let peace begin with me, let this be the moment now..."

All we need to do is continue our willingness to go beyond monitoring our thoughts and be conscious of what words we use in conversation with one another, and with ourselves. Our own self-talk is very important to become aware of.

We are all connected. Our words affect each other. We can now begin to feel compassion as we practice forgiving the words of others that cause damage. We can't control the negativity that devastates the atmosphere when it comes out of someone else's mouth. The path takes us to the middle ground. We can forgive aggression. We can face the pain. This takes courage on our part. We can reduce our ignorance by becoming more conscious of what speech does in our lives.

Today we meditate for twenty-six minutes. Before we begin, take a moment to reflect on your experience with words. Are your conversations filled with negative or positive words? Are they neutral? Do you talk to yourself with kindness or with self-criticism? Most of us live with too much negativity, with words that hurt rather than heal. This is reality, but it is a condition we can change our attitudes about.

I have learned that working with language takes time and practice. When someone speaks harshly to me, I try not to respond right away. I take a breath. Is this person upset about something else? Often, that is the case. I can walk away without responding. If I am feeling triggered, this is much harder to do, but it is the best way to prevent an altercation. I know how to calm myself, and this person may not know how to do that. So, I practice compassion. I go to the middle ground: not being aggressive, nor pushing away the pain I might feel from the person's words. I know that for me, when I am angry, I am often covering for fear or hurt. So, I can feel for everyone concerned. I do my best to expand my level of consciousness to the big picture. We are all connected.

The wisdom we have gained to this point involves a process called "practicing these principles in all of our affairs." We can now live an emotionally sane life in the world. When I forgive others and myself, when I practice kindness with my words, I do my part to have meaningful, respectful relationships. I focus on my own efforts; I keep my side of the street clean.

What helps you feel connected to others?

_____

_____

_____

_____

_____

_____

_____

_____

_____

_____

_____

_____

January 23rd

BRICK BY BRICK, WE BEGIN adding to the foundation of a new way of life. Moving deeper into our practice, we become conscious of the difference between action and reaction. A moment of action comes from the space of being with the breath, and is self-fulfilling. It needs no additions or subtractions because it just is. Reaction to any given situation of the moment comes from a place of want. It is co-dependent, out of balance, and creates a chain reaction of discursiveness that feeds our discontent.

A life of action brings peace. We take our raw emotions along with us, opening our hearts and minds to new wisdom that may be bestowed upon us. The focus is not on what could be learned; it is just being with our feelings, watching our thoughts as an observer, letting go, and making decisions to turn our wills and our lives over to the care of a higher power. We act from a place of vastness. We also act from a place of emptiness: there is no preconceived idea as to what the outcome may be. We encounter a new steadfastness that anchors us further to life in the present moment. We experience community in a new way.

Today we will meditate for twenty-seven minutes. Let's focus on your community: your family, your neighborhood, your city, and the world. So many things happen every day within these communities. And how we act and respond in our communities has a ripple effect. What kind of effect do you want to have in your family, your neighborhood, your city and in the world?

Meditation has taught us to be aware without judgment, and how to be calm within a storm. We get to practice responding differently to the people who are important to us. When someone does something that upsets us, we don't have to react. We can observe and we can do the next right thing, without confrontation.

If someone I know throws trash, I can observe him and see that he's upset about something. I can pick up the trash very peacefully and put it in the trash can. I do this because I have the ability to do so - and the consciousness as well. I do not spend time lecturing the person who dropped the paper. He's probably unconscious of this behavior right now. Another person may see me pick up the trash quietly. I picked up the paper because of my desire to be good toward the community. I acted compassionately. As a result, it may change the people who witnessed the action. All they see will be my non-judgmental attitude and my deed. I can do this now because I'm connected to the man who threw the trash through the feeling of compassion.

I change what I can. I change my reaction into an action. Without focusing on any outcome, I can gain the respect of a person watching me do the right thing. As I breathe in, I accept any discomfort about what I am observing, and I breathe out compassion for myself and my community. I am taking my practice from my room and trying it out in my life today.

Am I aware of how I relate to discomfort today? What do I do with that discomfort?

_____

_____

_____

_____

_____

_____

_____

_____

_____

_____

_____

_____

_____

_____

January 24th

As we check the six physical points of meditation - our seat, torso, legs, hands, eyes, and mouth - we can use our consciousness of intention, speech, and action to create a new life, one present moment at a time. We move away from what our ego wants to what our higher selves have to offer, which is an ever-expanding understanding of what we need as a connected society.

Creating a space in our minds through meditation allows us to open up to a new way of life one small step at a time. Our intention is to not have expectations. Our inner speech is something we merely observe during and after our center of meditation. We become the observer of our thoughts and actions, to see where we are opening up and where we are closing down. Gradually, we start to make small changes in the way we contribute to life, wherever we are. We move away from craving what we need and become more generous to ourselves and to those around us.

Bo Lozoff, the founder of the Human Kindness Foundation, says something very simple that gives us an idea of how to be conscious in our lives. He says, "Do your own time!" He wrote a book entitled, *We're All Doing Time*. Yes, people who are incarcerated have dissatisfactions, and so do we, every day. People on the street suffer through excessive thinking, speaking in ways that create

more pain, and reacting to others in a way that can cause a host of dramatic fiascos.

We've reached twenty-eight minutes today. Simply by taking our seat every day and increasing our practice one minute longer on a daily basis, we become guided by the larger picture that the space we create in our minds provides. Living our best life means focusing on being conscious long term. We move forward being with, and contribute to, life.

As you prepare for meditation today, what is on your mind? Use this space below to write down notes about your progress, so far. Are you making changes in your life that you feel good about? If not, take a moment to breathe. During your meditation today, ask for guidance.

_____

_____

_____

_____

_____

_____

_____

January 25th

OUR MEDITATION PRACTICE BRINGS US closer to dealing with pain, not further away. Yet, if we only strive to dive brutally into the fire, we'll be burned up before we reach any kind of enlightenment. We must also practice with ease. It's a lot like Goldilocks and the Three Bears – let's not be too hard on ourselves, not too soft - just right!

We sit in our practice to do our best, not too much or too little, with a particular idea in mind. We bring who we are, with all our faults and assets, while we act with faith - a willingness to face adversity for what it is with a compassion that arises without effort. We make friends with the darkest parts of ourselves. We change our perspective by opening to the larger truth that we all have something to contribute to this life, no matter where we come from.

We don't know what's in store in the future. We cannot change what is in the past. It takes courage to live in the present moment. We must learn to be gentle with ourselves. This is living in balance. We sit aside what the spiritual teachers call "the razor's edge" which represents the obstacles we must carefully cross to reach the path to enlightenment. By practicing gentle steadfastness, we learn to approach life gradually, with gratitude, and openness. We learn "to eat the elephant of life one bite at a time" - one thought, one feeling, and one moment at a time.

As we sit today in meditation for twenty-nine minutes, let's focus on how we approach life. Some of us charge into the day, ready to take on every project or take on the world. Some of us are quieter and prefer to observe, and possibly procrastinate. The path to serenity and enlightenment is in between. To find it and follow it, we need to be not too active or too passive. We need to be mindful and at ease. This is what we practice for.

I'm an overachiever. I am aware that I overdo. As I meditate today, I will leave these thoughts on the breath. Taking on more than my share of the responsibility for any situation is something I will lay at the altar of the present moment. Doing too much comes from a place of deficit, where I want to control the outcome of any situation because I cannot control another area of my life. Can you relate to that? I feel powerless over my need, my craving, to fix people and to fix the world. I've learned that when I try to control or manage other people or events, I'm the one who gets burned in the process. I will take a step back today, giving space to my discomfort in not being able to control peaceful outcomes.

I propose that today, if we are feeling passive, let's sit with our fear and self-doubt. And if we are feeling the need to control others, let's sit with self-righteousness, the other side of imbalance.

Remember that this practice takes courage. I have learned to ask for help from those I have learned to trust over the years. I practice patience to let any uncertainty unfold gently. When I was working on this book, I would sometimes feel blocked. So, I would just sit with that realization, accept the fact that I was stuck, and then breathe and wait for inspiration.

This is what we do in meditation. We keep coming back to the breath to go one step further into faith, one stride toward being enough, just for today. We realize we are not the only ones facing uncertainty or pain. Everyone faces emotional turmoil. You are not alone! I take the position of becoming the observer of my life, waiting to see what may come in the door in each present moment.

Let's make a pledge today to be open to soft spiritual growth. Focus on one thing you'd like to finish today. Then, give it away, unconditionally, to your higher power who will guide you through.

_____

_____

_____

_____

_____

_____

_____

_____

_____

_____

_____

_____

January 26th

MINDFULNESS IS THE PROCESS OF filling up our hearts while being present in ways that anchor us further to the present moment. Being with the breath is the groundbreaking of the construction of a temple within us. This is the open, quiet place within us where we are softly aware. We can go to this place inside us where we feel our emotions of fear, loneliness, anger, guilt, shame, and sadness.

If we get lost in thought, we can come back to the breath again and again. We practice letting go, emptying our minds and ourselves. Imagine pouring out a cupful of an old way of life, leaving nothing in its place. If it fills back up with familiar, self-defeating thoughts and habits, we must empty the cup over and over again. With that emptiness comes a vast array of wisdom that exists in our inner space, in the unmanifested. Wisdom that has been waiting to fill and proclaim who we are.

Silence and the progressive awareness of our being requires being present for ourselves. This is mindfulness. We create space inside us and soak up that vastness and emptiness. We don't try to define it. We just are. We sit and we are gently aware of our thoughts and our bodies.

Today as you meditate for thirty minutes, don't think your way into a solution; just stay present with whatever is.

On Saturdays, I go to the spiritual gym after I eat lunch. Saturdays are not workdays for me, so I make a point of resting and meditating. In my meditation chair or on my bed, I listen to the sounds in my house, letting go of judgment. I observe my body and my feelings.

I meditate for thirty minutes, and then I stretch. I feel how my body reacts to sitting. I do another thirty minutes. I gently bring myself back when I become lost in thought. It's just "thinking."

I have come to realize that wisdom comes randomly. I just have to be open in order to receive it. I could miss something important if I shut down my meditation time. That's a thought, so I let that go. By being in my spiritual gym, I am connected to the whole. My awareness strengthens my willingness to gently go to the space within, where compassion and kindness can be practiced.

What is some unexpected wisdom that has come to you?

_____

_____

_____

_____

_____

_____

_____

January 27th

NOW THAT WE HAVE LEARNED the basics of meditation, our focus becomes being present for any element that comes into our lives. We have learned techniques to practice living life from the inside out, rather than reacting from the outside in. We are creating clearer seeing and compassion, which will help us respond to whatever or whomever comes our way.

Whatever passes in front of us is the teacher and we are the students. Everything we experience we will use to till and fertilize the soil of our souls. In this way, we can rise above the existence of suffering to a spiritual perspective of progressive expansion.

Today, we will meditate for thirty-one minutes. We will go deeper into our practice. Today, I sit with anger and impatience. Then I go further: I realize this might not be an easy day for my family, either. They have their own struggles I may know nothing about. I may feel angry and impatient about what someone has done, but I have learned that when I feel the rage of resentment, I am the one drinking poison while I wait for the other person to suffer. So I go back to my breath and send the healing energy of compassion and tender loving-kindness to my family.

I send love from my open space within, and then send it outward, all the way to the mountains beyond my town.

Today, I spend my time taking care of myself. I shower, and I've had something to eat. I take a nap. No matter what is going on with my family members or my friends or colleagues, I can remain peaceful until I prepare for bed.

As we meditate today, let's focus on continuing to breathe no matter what is happening outside our rooms, our homes, or our towns. Let's remember the gentle wisdom that comes to us when we are peaceful. By reading this book, you are connecting with me and with all of the spiritual sages who have come before us and live among us today. As I meditate, I think, "Thank you Pema Chodron, I'm listening to you."

What is on your mind and heart today? Is there someone or something that is causing you to feel fear, loneliness, anger, guilt, shame, or sadness?

_____

_____

_____

_____

_____

_____

_____

_____

January 28th

FROM THE SPACE OF BALANCE come opportunities to be coached in patience. Grasping at what we want comes from believing that a person, place or thing will settle all our desires. That's a very narrow view of life. It is an ego truth and that brings us back to pain and powerlessness. If we concentrate on why we're impatient, we're looking at the object, instead of the impatient mind.

Now, let's continue to go inward, deeper into the simple idea that the mind feeds impatience with thought. Today, as we meditate for thirty-two minutes, let's just be with the impatient mind - letting go of the thoughts that fuel our irritation. What do you do when you're feeling impatient? I grind my teeth. But coming to grips with this awareness doesn't stop me right away. I may quietly pause the motion and come to rest, but sooner or later, I start up again. Gently, I come back to the breath and look at my impatience *instead of* my action of grinding my teeth, or *why* I am feeling impatient. I am developing patience by looking directly at the feeling, instead of trying to control the gnashing of my teeth or the reason I am doing it.

These are thoughts, so I let them go and just sit with the energy of impatience. I am aware that I get very impatient with myself. That's a thought that feeds grinding my teeth. So I let that go and breathe out compassion for myself, while relaxing my jaw.

The Buddha expressed the wisdom that we can turn arrows into flowers. I understand this proverb in a simple way. When I meditate, I can turn something that upsets me into something that nourishes my growth. And so can you.

What is upsetting you today? Can you see it as an opportunity to grow in awareness and wisdom?

_____

_____

_____

_____

_____

_____

_____

_____

_____

_____

January 29th

OUR EGOS ARE SHORTSIGHTED. THIS self-centered focus is narrow and often hypocritical. Seeing out is seeing the bigger picture. Instead of getting rid of the ego, we can be curious about the idea that we're all connected. If we do not understand the larger concept now, we can use this opportunity to experiment with creating a new way of life.

We can ask big questions, like, "Does unconditional love already exist within us, within our presence of being?" Creation, Love, and Being are all deeper levels of consciousness that we come to experience. They already exist deep within us. We've just forgotten them, because of our narrow egoical view.

It's hard to see the bigger picture when we feel pain. Dissatisfaction is filled with discordant opposites. To admit that we feel pain encourages us to take a step out of our comfort zone, outward and upward. This is a step toward spiritual awakening. We do not assume we will have a more panoramic view. This is an external, narrow perspective. Joy comes from within. We already have it. We just have to keep coming back to the breath to be open to sense it as it is. We become aware of how joy deepens on its own.

As we sit and meditate for thirty-three minutes today, let's focus on what is within us. Unconditional love already exists within us. We don't have to strive for it. There is a benevolence within.

Clear-seeing lets me know that bad things do happen, but I can only take responsibility for myself. The poem "Desiderata" by Max Ehrman reminds us not to compare ourselves to with others: "If you compare yourself with others, you may become vain or bitter, for always there will be greater and lesser persons than yourself."

Just breathe. All is well in this moment.

How has comparing yourself with others limited your growth in life?

_____

_____

_____

_____

_____

_____

_____

_____

_____

January 30th

WE UNDERSTAND AND NAVIGATE LIFE well when we meditate and go inside ourselves. Here is where we start with an awareness of our current state of consciousness. We make friends with this level and start where we are.

Current psychological thought about addiction is that the roots of all addictions are codependency in relationships and a lack of inward consciousness. Codependency is an excessive reliance on another person, resulting in an unhealthy, one-sided relationship. This includes a tolerance of harmful behavior. Often, people with addictions are in codependent relationships without realizing it. This is very common, and something to learn about as we grow in self-acceptance and practice new behaviors.

Once we realize we are codependent, our minds become the managers of our reactions and we can start to develop curious, compassionate friendship with whatever inner feeling state we experience during meditation.

If we are resentful, fearful, or self-righteous in a relationship, we start with that awareness. We accept where we are. We gently make a decision to turn our focus from listening to our narrowly focused minds to the outward breath. We replace our thoughts with a kind, repeated mantra such as, "I am okay. I am safe." Or, "I am loving-kindness."

Our intention is not to grasp at life's potential for our own satisfaction or joy, but to be present to what is. Setting a goal to be the kindest, most peaceful person in any relationship is focusing on an external outcome. So, we focus instead on the moment and breathe.

Keeping it simple, we sit in meditation to exercise our conscious understanding, while moving toward a peaceful conclusion to all matters. We continue to practice looking clearly at what is, while adding whatever compassion and kindness we have available at the time.

We will sit and meditate for thirty-four minutes today. Let's focus on understanding and accepting ourselves, and then being open to becoming the best version of ourselves.

What does that look like to you?

_____

_____

_____

_____

_____

_____

January 31ˢᵗ

Increasing our consciousness through meditation on a daily basis is the way we arrive at spiritual awakening. The three concepts of meditation, consciousness, and spiritual awakening, are built into the fabric of all Twelve-Step Programs, starting with Alcoholics Anonymous, which was formed in 1939.

We can begin our journey toward spiritual awakening by seeing ourselves more honestly. The direction of the journey is to see inward, but away from the selfish ego, which is often the focus of an addict.

In quiet contemplation, we experience inner calm through a sequential awareness of our physical body and our place in the world; however, our search is to simply "be," which is not of this world. Every living creature has an invisible life force. This energy connects us all. We strive to live in balance with one another.

One of the goals of reflection is to see beyond the self to the cumulative connective domain. Each day we practice, we start anew. We are freshly charged with what we gain from the empty space we create within. There is nothing measurable to gain; wisdom is not spiritual covetousness. The pause in our day when we meditate gives us a chance to turn away from any immediate reaction toward a conscious choice to turn our will over to the power greater than ourselves. This is the basic idea in Step Three of any Twelve-Step Program.

Today is the last day of January. We will sit and meditate for thirty-five minutes, focusing on gratitude. Let's appreciate our inner life force that carries us even when we are tired or discouraged. And let's thank our higher power for the guidance we receive during meditation.

What would you like to say to your higher power? Who would you like to thank for their patience and guidance?

_____

_____

_____

_____

_____

_____

_____

_____

_____

_____

_____

_____

February 1st

LET'S BRING THE IDEA OF failure into our practice. We've all failed at something. Meditation allows us to look at the higher purpose for failure. We don't just give up. We bring the feelings of hopelessness, shame, and guilt to the cushion; we sit to find our way to humility. We ask what we can learn from our failure.

We all are truly connected; no one is better than anyone else. Failure can be the seed that blossoms into something that changes us for the better. And as we improve, we can be the change in our families, our communities, and the world. The choice is ours.

The spiritual perspective on worldly failure depends on what choices we make now. We start by helping ourselves. We face our pain head on, developing a faith in a higher purpose that connects us. Once our cup is filled up, the humility we learn can be given away to others. We let go of any outcome.

Today we will meditate for thirty-six minutes. We cannot change the past. Our failures may bring us to great sadness. I feel sad when I can't undo what I've done, or when the world does not understand or forgive me. That's a thought, so I drop it and sit with the sadness.

My meditation practice comes from admitting that I am powerless over what the world thinks of me. Other people's opinions of me are none of my business. I can turn self-doubt into the seed that stabilizes my mind. I can take self-righteousness and use my failure to humble me to the point where I am equal to every other human being on earth.

In this practice, I am going into my inner space, opening up to the idea that everyone has a higher self that deserves love. Everyone! I open myself up to feeling compassion. I surrender to the possibility of tender loving-kindness. I may have failed, but I am not a failure.

What pain and suffering can you breathe through and let go of today?

_____

_____

_____

_____

_____

_____

_____

_____

_____

_____

February 2ⁿᵈ

WE LIVE OUR WHOLE LIVES using our five senses - sight, hearing, touch, smell, and taste. Our thinking about what we sense keeps us locked into experiencing life in the physical sense; however, using the sixth sense, the ability to be conscious of what we do from the viewpoint of who we are, adds the dimension of wisdom to our lives. Wisdom is greater than the knowledge gained through our base mind.

We practice meditation to distill our ability to quiet our mind and bring it to our presence. Spiritual acquisition is not the goal; such an ambition is not obtainable. We follow the path by seeing what is. What happens is an expanded vision arising in the present moment. Christians call this being reborn, becoming the truth of Christ's life example. Let's be open to the possibility that living in the present moment is what allowed Jesus to be free from sin. Going eastward, this is the same refined introspection exemplified by the practice of the Buddha, the enlightened one.

This soul searching is the foundation for mindfulness - observing our thoughts, emotions, our body sensations, our breath, and ultimately our ability to let go of outcomes as a more wide-open response to grief.

Today we will meditate for thirty-seven minutes. When I am on the street, I have all of my five senses and my ability to be conscious. I can use these anchors to bring me to now. Now is not dependent on where I am. It is being aware of who I am. I have become aware of my higher self. I have the space and the time to practice sitting with my breath as often as I choose, wherever I choose.

My practice helps me to gently stop reacting to the things I see that don't meet my mind's expectation of perfection. My hearing is still pretty good. Being aware of sounds as I sit and breathe allows me to sense that sound has a beginning and an end. No sound goes on forever. The moments of silence that happen in my practice are the seeds of a new way of being.

There are good smells and bad smells. They, too, come and go. I have the opportunity to taste when I eat. I'm grateful to taste an apple almost every day. That's a simple gift. When I exercise, I move better. I feel better. I get to sit with my body, becoming more aware of how to be gentler with myself throughout the day. I am aware of my breath, not just on the meditation pillow. I catch myself being aware of my breath throughout the day.

Feel free to write down any actions you can take to be gentler with yourself that may come to you.

_____

_____

_____

_____

_____

February 3rd

WHEN DO WE PRACTICE? THE answer is simple: when it's most practical. When is there less noise to get started? Perhaps we can wake up early enough that the morning is quiet enough to start our practice. If that doesn't work, we can choose a time in the evening, after the family has settled down for the night. The key is to be gentle with ourselves, while seeing more clearly. Everything we do in our practice comes from two points: clear-seeing and compassion toward the middle ground. We live in a world of duality. Our mission is to work with it.

We also have to take into account what kind of job we have and what times we have to go to work. There might be time during our day's work that we're not doing anything at all. What a perfect time to practice. In the beginning, we don't try to practice when it's loud and there's a lot of movement. We're just getting started. Tenderness must accompany discovery. Peace isn't right or wrong, it just is!

I find the period just after midnight is a great time for me to sit and practice. There is silence at this hour in my home. Very few people move during this time of day. I work in the afternoon, so midnight is a perfect time for me. I sit comfortably on my pillow, positioned on my bed. The faint lights in my house create a gray haze.

I can hear my heartbeat because it is so quiet. When I am still, I can feel the pulses throughout my body. I add something to my practice tonight. I call it a mantra. When I breathe out, I say "I". When I breathe in, I say "AM". On the inward breath, I let go. The spirit part of me is vast and empty - indefinable. Coming back to the outward breath, I have an awareness that keeps me focused. If I wander away, I just come back on the outgoing breath, while being present for my body, my breath, and any emotions that arrive. After my thirty-eight minutes, I lie down and continue the mantra until I fall asleep.

What is a mantra you can say to yourself while you meditate?

_____

_____

_____

_____

_____

_____

_____

_____

_____

February 4th

MAKING FRIENDS WITH OUR THOUGHTS is worth our attention. Obsessive dialogue within creates emotional intensity, or procrastination and negligence. When we overthink, the focus is outward, so we can only observe what our thinking is doing to cloud our minds.

Our compulsive thinking brings us to miss the mark, instead of processing and letting go of negative feelings such as fear, loneliness, anger, guilt, shame, and sadness. Meditation allows us to be present with our thoughts, making them our friends by saying "thinking" aloud, and then being clear enough to turn our attention to our breath. We can begin to see thoughts as impermanent and not solid. Moment by moment, even intense emotional energy can be resolved.

Just practicing meditation sets us up to turn away from our compulsive lack of consciousness; we repent - another overused Christian word. Again, let's use a light, airy approach and endorse the idea of repentance as thinking again, a reflection that has a broader, wiser essence. The larger perspective leads us to hit the mark: we can experience our feelings with our feet firmly planted in the meditation space until the energy passes. This new expression of faith has no goal. Simply being with what is. There is only the path.

We are meditating for thirty-nine minutes today. I am making friends with my compulsive mind. The sages tell me not to beat myself up for getting carried away in my thoughts, my ego's reflection. Chogyam Trungpa Rinpoche and Pema Chodron both speak of "touching thoughts with a feather," then letting them go. That's a simple theory to become gently curious about. There is no goal to be thought-free!

I put my confidence and trust in the space of unconditional love. I bring all of my painful, raw feelings and dump them into the gap of silence. I ask my great sadness to sit with me, right here on the bed. It's ok to feel sad. And I am not the only person feeling this way. These are thoughts I can befriend. I touch them lightly and let them go.

I am never alone. When I pray, I feel close to my higher power who I call God. Here is a prayer I say.

God, I love you with all my heart. You are inside me. Forgive me and forgive us all. I am committed to facing my pain and dropping it in faith and with hope. I'm not asking you to take away my dissatisfaction, only to help me to make better decisions based on your wisdom. I turn my will over to your care.

I realize we all deserve unconditional love. I'm no different. I open my heart and let go! Good night!

Feel free to write your prayer or your reflections here.

_____

_____

_____

_____

February 5th

TODAY, WE HAVE REACHED OUR meditation goal of forty minutes! Let's explore the phrase "I want" more deeply today. This need to control outcomes, to have our way, and to be self-absorbed, is called narcissism. We use narcissistic behavior to make pain go away, but it only removes us further from who we really are.

Meditation, the means to clarify all present moments with wisdom, brings us to the understanding that "I", "ME" and "MINE" are all illusions that bring great anguish. Selfishness is a corrupted attempt to solve the wrong problem from the wrong end. The wisdom of the present moment helps us to focus on the process, not the outcome. This is an inward process, not outward grasping.

Underneath the drive of self-centered behavior is the desire to appease what our culture defines as "negative emotions". We desperately want negative emotion to go away. We want to end the suffering caused by strong feelings such as fear, loneliness, anger, guilt, shame, sadness, abandonment…. and the list goes on and on.

What happens when we stop the discursive thoughts that feed these emotions? Let's experiment with the phrase, "I Have". Perhaps creating a gap of silence will help us to change directions, allowing the wisdom of "I Have" to arise. This is an attitude of gratitude. We do two things when we focus on what we have: we realize what we're truly grateful for, and we replace what we want with what we have.

1. We begin to see clearly that strong emotions, which we reflexively move away from, are worth moving towards. We make these painful emotions our friends. We invite them into the space we create.

2. We begin to become more compassionate with ourselves and, through opening up, we come to realize our connection to others. We start to share, instead of take, through our awareness. We see that all of us face these emotions. There is no "I" to be selfish about. Compassion is always there; we have it. We already have the capacity to be fulfilled.

Upon reaching today's goal of forty minutes, we can choose this process for the rest of the book series, or we can break up the time frames into two twenty-minute sessions during the day. Remember, mindfulness can be done while walking, taking a bath, or even riding the metro. As we do, let's think about what we are grateful for.

What are you grateful for today?

_____

_____

_____

_____

_____

February 6th

SOMETIMES WHEN I SIT STILL, the wisdom that arises is the concept of relativity. How we perceive any instance depends on what we compare it to, or what we have experienced in the past. We judge things based on where we are in the world of duality. Black is relatively dark next to gray; however, gray is relatively dark next to white. So, what is gray? When it's paired with black, it's lighter; but when it's paired with white, it's darker. When our awareness moves above the necessity for such evaluation, we can see clearly and let go of the dual perspective in favor of the absolute in the spiritual realm. Black just is. Gray just is. White just is!

1. We are learning to allow The Universe to speak for itself, instead of drawing our own conclusions. From a scientific point of view, meditation reshapes our brains. Many years ago, it was thought that one could not change one's brain at all. Now, new studies show that the brain can change. Meditation has brought a new flexibility. Things are not cast in stone, as once believed. We can learn to face problems in a new way:

2. We don't draw a target to mark a conclusion.

3. We go from the mind to the heart.

4. We begin to see each a teachable moment as a moment to wake up.

5. **We start seeing moments as impermanent, while the spirit of consciousness is eternal.**

Today, I choose to observe. Instead of circular thinking, which happens when I am ruminating about the past or the future, I choose to listen to my breath. I'm anchoring to the present moment. Rather than focusing on what has happened or what will happen tomorrow, I choose to sense this moment. When thoughts or emotions arise, I say "thinking" and return to the breath. Whatever I am worried about is not happening right now, in this moment. I can breathe slowly and calmly, and I can repeat the comforting mantra, "This too shall pass."

Practice saying, "This too shall pass" every time an upsetting thought arises. How does that help you sit with the pain without compulsively thinking about the problem?

_____

_____

_____

_____

_____

_____

_____

February 7th

MEDITATION BRINGS SANITY BECAUSE IT allows us to reach toward the vast emptiness above the physical world through presence. We submit our full participation with all of our six avenues of familiarity - sight, sound, smell, touch, and taste. And we add the mindfulness of simply our presence.

There is a relationship between consciousness and the physical. The spiritual cannot exist without the physical and the physical cannot exist without the spiritual. There is a phrase that makes it simple: form is emptiness and emptiness is form. Whether it's the alpha and the omega or Ying/Yang there is no separation. It's like trying to solve the problem of which came first - the chicken or the egg. I AM is simply what is. There is birth, and then there is death.

"I" is not solid, yet it is interrelated to every existing thing. All of us are bound by consciousness. We come to the meditation cushion to observe and accept ourselves, whether we are obsessive-compulsive in our thoughts, or we have other difficulties. We don't push thoughts away. We make a direct acquaintance with them without grabbing hold of them. We gently peel back the thought and let it go, to experience the feeling state underneath, without being moved off our balance.

Thoughts are not permanent. Owning thoughts is the root of our dissatisfaction. We take our thoughts as personal statements.

This practice is about not taking anything personally. We just watch what rolls into our mind and watch those thoughts dissolve.

Today, I focus on an image within my mind to emphasize that all of time is impermanent. I'm sitting in a field. It is a bright, sunny day with only a few clouds. I sit and I check my posture. I observe my seat, legs, torso, hands, eyes, and mouth. A cloud moves and the sun disappears for a while. This is thought. I observe it with clear-seeing and gentleness as I say, "thinking" and wait for it to pass. The sun comes out again, and I think it's there for me.

I tend to make all life experiences personal. I falsely identify with my ego. The clouds are distractions, like thoughts that come and go. I spend the rest of my session clearly seeing and being with my outward breath, letting go of any cloud that comes in my stream of consciousness.

A Buddhist saying is, "Let the world speak for itself." The power of now gives me the opportunity to pause and give space to allow things to unfold before I start making guesses about what I believe is going on.

What are you noticing in your environment today? What do you think the world is trying to tell you?

_____

_____

_____

_____

February 8th

WITH EVERY DAY THAT PASSES, something inevitably goes wrong within any given moment. The natural human response is to take hold of pleasure and to move away from the pain.

Through practicing meditation, we begin to look at any given instance, whether pleasurable or agonizing, and question its highest truths:

1. If each moment is separate in terms of our experience, is any moment lasting or impermanent?

2. Is the person, place, or thing causing uneasiness able to, in any moment, sustain this hurtful episode?

3. Does identifying with the trouble ease or increase with our involvement? And with whom is this supposedly permanent self having this experience?

A single answer repeatedly comes from meditation: everything is impermanent. We often react to persons, places, and things, but nothing is everlasting. Identifying with the permanent self escalates pain. In the spiritual realm, we are all connected through whatever we encounter. We are all spiritual beings having a human experience.

During meditation, coming back to my breath in the present moment represents being inquisitive about the highest truth. I see that my ego wants to hold onto and solve every single, painful moment that comes across my path. Focusing on my breath allows me to live in each separate experiential moment. All of the thoughts I have about people, places, or things that create uneasiness within me just arise. Making the decision to come back to the breath allows me to let go of any sustained reaction. This too shall pass.

My ego is not going to miraculously dissolve. I am learning to watch it with as clear eyes as is possible in any given moment, while being gentle and kind to myself. This dual solution, dealing with the duality of the world of form, allows me to go to the middle ground that exists in the silence that arises. The physical world has opposites: tall/short, fat/thin, black/white. This is duality. The middle ground is the place of balance between the two opposites in duality. This small pause allows me the patience I need to act out the best possible decision now.

As I meditate, I am learning to practice, in daily life, what I am doing on the cushion. I am watching as the haze of ache arises when I react to someone, something, or someplace that offends the illusions of my ego. I am committed to my practice, not just for me, but for anyone who picks up this book to conduct this experiment with me.

When you pause today, notice what your middle ground looks and feels like. What do you observe?

_____

_____

_____

February 9th

No one likes being told what to do. The reaction is often anger. Instead of looking at the two-dimensional picture of who is wrong and who is right, the mindful meditation panorama moves us toward wisdom, rather than knowledge.

Knowledge is cut and dried, black or white. It is judgment, relying on established societal facts and norms. Wisdom, on the other hand, relies on going to the space of quiet, trusting in first-hand experience as the guiding factor for making decisions. To judge someone as right or wrong is a state of ego, of knowledge. In spacious awareness, we observe the behavior of others without judgment.

We don't accept what is handed to us, but instead, we give what is before us a mindful focus to come to believe in the highest truth. Wisdom connects us, where knowledge may separate us.

This wisdom we seek can be found inside the practice of observing and pausing. We undergo a transformation, from resistance to acceptance, through our willingness to open our hearts to first-hand instruction.

Through meditation, our relationship with a person who relies on knowledge and judgment switches from what is true or false to what is observed. Once we are clear that another's mental state is not conscious, that it is not coming from a higher level, the place of wisdom, we understand that trying to change them or dispute them makes us just as unconscious. What people do changes from moment to moment. Who they are is never to be judged as right or wrong. If we are not conscious, we confuse who we are with what we do. The key is to be present and remain neutral.

When I encounter someone who is demanding or judgmental, I take a breath, just as in my practice, and I try to gently move myself above judgment of his actions in an effort to be aware of what needs to be done in the present moment. If the interaction is intense or hostile, I say, "I need to go," and I step away. I practice not taking his anger personally. Later, I may ask him to clarify, in writing, what he was saying. I am staying away from who is right and who is wrong, I ask only to clarify. My experiment with not judging is practicing, in real life, what I do on the cushion. I am looking at a more expanded perspective.

Write down your thoughts here. If someone upsets you, could you see that it may have nothing to do with you? Could you take a step back?

_____

_____

_____

_____

_____

_____

February 10th

THERE IS A WISE SAYING that performing any activity continuously for more than thirty days will move that activity into a habit status. Meditation is a verb, not a noun, and an action worthy of daily practice.

In our choice to pause, meditation becomes an activity where boundless joy may arise. We experience a sense of gratitude. We begin to see that happiness occurs when we exist within a genuine acceptance of what is. Finally, we make life meaningful through our efforts of generosity, compassion, and kindness.

Through a clear-seeing inventory of ourselves, and by surrounding ourselves with compassion, we come to see everything around us as equal. Good is something to enjoy and give away. Bad is an opportunity to stay grounded and add our goodwill until it passes. We all have character flaws and assets worthy of introspection. Our focus becomes our increased awareness of our thoughts, words, and deeds, and how they affect the whole.

To have a life of balance, we work on ourselves because that is the sole driving force for selflessness. Ego is an illusion; we are not separate beings. Everything we do affects the whole human experience. Understanding this truth brings us to enjoy boundless happiness and a meaningful life.

We are practicing how to live a life of unconditional love. The habit of opening up just a bit more every day and allowing whatever enters our life to go directly to our heart, instead of regurgitating it in our mind, is the core of our practice.

I give my practice forty minutes. I can break it up into two different sessions, if I wish. This is my personal spiritual vitamin that I am choosing to take each day. I am developing a sense of what is not material. I spend each day strengthening my use of compassion, tender loving-kindness, joyful exertion and equanimity, no matter what walks into my practice. Everything is an opportunity to grow.

Choose someone to share your compassion and tender-loving care with. What is that experience like for you?

_____

_____

_____

_____

_____

_____

_____

_____

February 11th

SITTING IN MEDITATION BRINGS US to wisdom as we strive to reach a state of spiritual ease. But it can also bring forth the awareness of ignorance that may be permeating our lives. An ignorant state can come in two forms – either by encountering something to which we've never been exposed, or a character defect we've incorrectly assumed is our truth.

When we probe deeper, if we have become aware of our own personality flaws, there lies a feeling state with which we can sit. In a state of reflection, we can accept that we are not perfect.

At that moment, we can become entirely ready to give up our imperfections to the space of meditation. As we do this, we set into motion our character assets of faith, hope, and love. Let's go easy on ourselves as we grow. It is only up to The Universe to reveal how truly flawed we are.

Self-doubt is my number-one character flaw. I see it clearly! Even when I "think" I'm right, I'm aware that I allow someone else to sway me into doubting what is in my heart. Self-doubt is crushing to the soul!

I've learned to ask for help when I am in self-doubt. I ask others I trust for their input, so that I stay true to myself and stop committing emotional self-abuse. I recognize that asking for help allows me to open up, instead of choosing isolation. I'm ready to put this defect on the chopping block. I'm letting it go!

What personality flaw would you like to get rid of? Write it down here and ask your higher power to take it from you.

_____

_____

_____

_____

_____

_____

_____

_____

_____

_____

_____

_____

February 12th

BALANCE OF THE MIND IN meditation can be joyfully achieved through music. Creating, listening, and performing music add to the experience. Just as the mind begins at rest, so the music begins with the staff, in treble or bass. Then the first tone, the tonic, presents itself. This is the key to music.

To find equilibrium in life and in music, we keep coming back to the point of rest. In musical arrangements, the wisdom is to always begin with the tonic and end with a particular note before resolving back to silence. The musical piece resembles our meditative practice. There are rests of silence amidst the scores of notes and words. Music and meditation inspire us to reach for a higher spiritual understanding.

Participating in a church choir is a form of music meditation, for me. Everything seems to disappear during rehearsal, as I learn, practice, and bring a new piece to fruition with the other members of the choir.

During church, when I sing, I can hear my voice as it distinctly adds to the message. I am also conscious of the ensemble of men in the choir. I focus on the music and the message, and how it affects my practice. I face pain with music. I don't try to make the pain go away while singing. I come to the present moment of discontent, transcended by the flow of emotional music.

One particular song is very meaningful to me, "Hold On." I see the notes dancing on the page as I hear the music and the message. I can smell and taste its meaning with my spiritual palette. I feel the beat on my skin as the wisdom of the words resounds in my ears, all of this combining to bring me to tears.

Do you have a special song or musical experience you can add to your meditation?

_____

_____

_____

_____

_____

_____

_____

_____

_____

_____

February 13th

WHEN WE GIVE OUR WILLINGNESS to our sitting practice, what we experience is how to remain in "the power of NOW", a phrase coined by Eckhart Tolle in his book, *The Power of NOW*. As we become more conscious, we realize that thoughts of the future or the past feed emotional disturbance - because we can change neither. In the presence of now, we develop the courage to change the things we can.

What develops next is our awareness of cause and effect. A classic example is the fact that the sun always rises in the east and sets in the west, never any other way - except on the occasion of a solar eclipse. What meditation brings to our attention is what we project is happening NOW, based on what we see, hear, smell, taste, and feel. We assume a lot, and often our prediction is dead wrong.

Instead of pushing away these unwanted projections or beliefs, we treat them the same way that we contemplate ruminations of the past and the future. We allow them to rise and fall like the tides.

What is of greater importance is becoming more alert to the way our emotions affect what we believe is reality. Often, we can be dulled to all that exists, run away from what is, or be thrown full throttle into a conclusion based on passion.

Our heightened feeling states such as fear, anger, or sadness are fed by compulsive thoughts and expectations that may or may not be true. The emotional pull within our minds may be compared to the static that occurs as we fine-tune a radio to get the best reception of a certain station.

Moving toward pain with a curious mind, while moving away from pleasure, allows us to increase the depths of our understanding and our reactive patterns. Without the objects or origins of our feelings as a focus, we can practice watching the energy of the emotion as it rises and falls.

I'm finding it takes courage to concentrate on the now when strong feelings arise. I know I can blow something all out of proportion with my compulsive thinking! My ego goes into full swing. I see how I'm not staying in the now. My mind wants to create a story where I win.

Over and over, it's important to stop, be gentle with ourselves, and kindly go back to feeling our feet on the floor. We don't have to react when we feel angry or upset. We can pause, notice a color in the room, and listen to our breath going in and out of our body.

Thinking about something positive helps. I recently observed someone doing something nice for someone else. I am grateful to watch such kindness. My mind says, "That kind of behavior is rare." And that's a thought, so I say, "thinking" and take a breath.

During meditation, we learn to lean into pain without a storyline. We don't think about why we feel a certain way, we just notice what we feel. For many of us, this is a new habit to create. When I find myself being carried away in mindless chatter, I have the opportunity to be with the feeling states I'm experiencing. Even if I'm only a tiny bit successful in coming back to the present moment of now, it's a start.

How can I sit with doubt, anger, or fear without using my thinking mind?

_____

_____

_____

_____

_____

_____

_____

_____

_____

_____

_____

_____

February 14ᵗʰ

ACTION THAT REFLECTS BEING BRINGS balance. This is equanimity - the middle way. Here, clear-seeing meets compassion, where natural joy arises. From this place of focus, we can observe the energy that comes up. We use this as a process, continuously coming back to the stillness of being.

In this place, things hidden become obvious for the first time, perhaps. Any situation can now come to a more visible space, even our stumbling blocks.

The closest we can come to who we are is by coming to our breath. This is the essence of our consciousness. Whether we believe we continue on past our death is irrelevant. What matters most is the moment of now that exists in each and every inhalation and exhalation. No matter our religious beliefs or our current spiritual understanding, everything starts with the breath of life.

In the midst of hungering for delight and avoiding discomfort, coming to the center of who we are, on the breath, is the process that brings us peace. In this place of harmony, we find balance. In this place of balance, we find peace.

Some days, meditation is difficult! Even with all of my reading and practice, if I am in pain or otherwise upset, kindness and compassion toward myself or others do not flow naturally. In the past, I used many things to make pain go away. This does not work for me anymore, so I tell myself to stop. I turn my focus away from the object or person of my discontent. I find a quiet place and I just sit with the ache of disappointment or upset. I expand my horizon to just be.

Instead of focusing just on me, I do my best to be aware, on my breath, of all the people in the world who do not reflexively feel compassion and kindness for themselves. I am connected by this principle. My ego wants to blame mostly myself, yet in the now, I've not done anything wrong. I am practicing as best I can. I am living in the middle, in the middle way. Thinking about the past or the future makes things worse for me. It's all just conjecture. I keep coming back to my breath.

What helps you let go of the past and future when you are meditating? How can you carry that ability into your daily life?

_____

_____

_____

_____

_____

_____

February 15th

As we come to the end of this foundation for practicing meditation, let's look at this hypothesis: Consciousness of the breath and the body, and our thoughts and feelings, allows the brain the perfect scenario for learning faith, hope, love, and being.

The scientific experiment to see if this hypothesis is true is "personally experiential." Only the individual can evaluate the wisdom of this theory. This is where science and the ethereal meet.

What we find, through our practice of sitting still, is the immeasurable expanse where wisdom can be found. Once we experience this space, we also perceive that we can never pinpoint its locale. It moves out of the physical world, into the spiritual, only to reappear in a different place, in its own time.

Wisdom is not an outcome, but an immersive process. It's not that its ultimate truth changes, but our moment-to-moment perspective is relative to that flow of energy.

What I have learned is that when I meditate, I experience peace. And when I am in a peaceful state, I am open to seeing things differently. I am open to learning a new way of being.

What are you learning as you continue with your practice? What feels new and better, now?

_____

_____

_____

_____

_____

_____

_____

_____

_____

_____

_____

_____

_____

_____

February 16th

EVERY MOMENT IS A TEACHER.

When I am aggressed upon, feelings of fear, anger, and possibly self-doubt arise. The wisdom I have learned in my practice is to give myself and my feelings space enough to make the most peaceful decision about how I may react.

The key is to stay centered and work the issue from the inside out. The answer is never between you and the other person. It is between you and the Universal mind. Time allows us to experiment with this. To respond aggressively is a basic tool of survival; however, addressing one's anger has many possibilities. Pausing long enough to be aware of anger is a courageous choice.

The idea of right and wrong is a very basic level of truth. There are higher choices of reasoning. Choosing to love oneself and one's neighbor takes practice. We can prepare for this by rehearsing these new choices in our minds, in advance.

When we become angry, our rational minds close down, and our options become limited. We need to pause. Stepping away from an intense interaction allows us to open up to a new experience of our anger. We can sense what is underneath that anger and find compassion and kindness for ourselves. We come to understand a new way to relate to the world.

I fear angry people. This horror goes back pretty far. This is in the past, though. I can break free of the chains of my own mind by concentrating and making friends with my fear when it arises. Instead of reacting to this fear with mental anguish and memories of past abuse, I just sit with the darkness of fear. I drop it in the space I create in meditation. I am making a decision to make progress in my life by allowing what I feel to simply be.

I am developing relaxation and open awareness. I see clearly. I allow the energy of compassion to flow as it wishes. Most things in life are not under my control. I slowly let go and allow God to show me how this works! I can't really love my neighbor unconditionally until I love who I am first!

As a child, I was told not to love myself, and that to do so is selfishness. That is a thought I have let go of. This is now! I am not looking at the person I believe causes my fear, but at fear itself, without an object. All I need is my breath to stay anchored.

What is the present moment teaching you about seeing more clearly today?

_____

_____

_____

_____

_____

_____

February 17th

The space that we create during meditation can be used after our practice. If we don't access our desired path, we can make a list of the mistakes we made and learn something new about ourselves.

Steadfastness comes with patience. Detachment with love allows those we have offended the time it takes to deal with their own feelings and discursive thoughts. We all have different paths. The only focus is on the course we are taking.

We all create splinters in our relationships. We all make mistakes; we all offend people at times, and they offend us. When someone expresses anger toward me, I back away quietly, even from the people I am close to, in order to see what happened more clearly, and to recognize my own patterns with friendships. What is my part in what just happened?

Sometimes we need to set boundaries with people who are angry with us. I can make the decision to detach from people who are angry with me.

Often, if we give the predicament some time and space, while breathing compassion and kindness in both directions – toward the other person and toward ourselves – we can find resolution.

I know I can also make a decision to continue my friendships with those I trust. I can choose to focus on those positive relationships. I can let go of that which I can't change, and I can find the courage to change the thing I can – me.

What is your experience with anger in the present moment?

_____

_____

_____

_____

_____

_____

_____

_____

_____

_____

_____

_____

_____

February 18th

WE ARE LEARNING THAT WHEN angry, there are many possibilities for response. If we pause long enough to accept the anger that has arisen within us, we can find the most peaceful way of transforming it for the good of the community. By creating that space, we can more clearly and honestly see the next step of action.

The address of the space where we find our God is not someplace in the sky. It is in the true heart, the highest place within us.

It always helps me to make a list of possible responses when I am feeling angry or hurt. Anger is the shield that covers hurt. We get angry to protect ourselves when we are hurt, to push people away. In meditation, my mind expands to see the ultimate truth. I come to know that beyond feeling angry, I feel hurt. I experience that feeling in my gut.

After I have meditated, I can make a decision to let the person know how their comment affected me, or not. I can choose my words carefully: "When you said that, I felt hurt." If this course of action does not create peace within me, I chalk it up to experience and I move on to the next moment with greater discernment.

This is the process of letting go and letting God, the empowerment of the spirit through experimentation. I vow to practice courage and discernment. Anger does not always require a response. It often requires self-care.

What happened the last time you got angry, or someone was angry with you? Can you identify your feelings underneath the angry encounter? How can you take care of yourself right now?

_____

_____

_____

_____

_____

_____

_____

_____

_____

_____

_____

_____

February 19th

OUR FEELINGS COME FROM WITHIN us. Our feelings are fed by our thoughts. Our thoughts fuel our words, and our words fuel our actions. Our actions become our patterns of behavior, our behavior determines our life's work, and our life's work determines our destiny.

In the physical world, in the sphere of knowledge, there are opposites – right and wrong, good and evil. We would not understand short without tall, or day without night. In the spiritual world, there are no opposites. What exists just is. There is no time. There is no space. Energy comes from this vacuum into the physical world and eventually goes back from where it came. What do we do with this energy we call feelings? Normally, we react to them when our ego is in control.

Let's take a look at the phrase "I am." If "I" is in the physical world, with our body, our flesh; then "am" must exist in the spiritual world. We can tell we are in this body. We can see ourselves in the mirror. The ego experiences time and space. When we experience the energy of a feeling state, our first reaction is to close down and protect "I."

Normally, our ego is in the foreground and the "am" part, the spiritual part, is in the background. But the "am" in us never changes. It just is. What if we moved the spiritual part, the part of us that is constant, to the foreground and the ego to the background? We

begin to observe ourselves. We begin to awaken. Our awareness expands our vision of the sacredness of The Universe. This starts with us, with "I" making a decision to surrender to consciousness.

Now is the moment to allow the spiritual to feed me, observing when I run into the walls of emotional pain located in the physical world. I understand that feelings are energy. I'm practicing allowing them to arise, like noticing an itch without scratching.

Now is the moment to accept my thoughts, and then let them go. I choose to call this "thinking" instead of giving my thoughts a positive or negative connotation. Sitting still to allow this energy to flow through me is a conversion from my mind to my heart. This allows me to let go of any judgment or reaction.

I'm sparsely aware of the words I use which come from my compulsive thoughts, but I know I can't stop them perfectly today. I have to experiment, watching what I think and observing what I say. Judgment comes from my thoughts and not my heart.

My faith and hope are that my words can change and that I can see what effect they have on my actions. The key lies in the focus of my consciousness, allowing this space to change my patterns of behavior. To me, this is going to the "spiritual gym." The process is slow. I'm not going to grow all the muscles I need by working out the first time.

This gentleness may be new for you, along with compassion. When I suddenly see a direction to take in my life, this is divine destiny that comes from within me. I look forward to my life flowing more smoothly, with a greater sense of fulfillment. All I need is a commitment to a willingness to practice.

For today, are you able to let go of your thoughts gently?

February 20th

IMAGINE THE POSSIBILITY THAT THERE is only one soul. We reject that idea since we're in separate bodies; we can't be connected. I believe we are all connected. When we judge one another, we're really judging ourselves. We are all worthy of the kindness and compassion that starts with an internal action.

If every human being is connected to a collective soul, then wisdom is the path that leads to human understanding. Coming to understand who we are takes time and discipline. There also has to be a large dose of gentleness in the discovery. We are our own worst critic. This sense of unworthiness commonly spills over into our lives while we are trying to control pain. Unfortunately, it usually only worsens the situation.

If someone criticizes us, we take it to heart. Perhaps it is time to practice the phrase, "Other people's opinions of me are none of my business." When we take on someone else's judgment, we take away their responsibility for their own path to wisdom. People judge what they recognize in themselves, without that awareness.

We learn to do this with the hope of steadfast faith. The practice of loving our neighbors as ourselves becomes easier when we recognize that they make the same mistakes we do. We can empathize. We must keep coming back to the mirror.

As you meditate today, think about what makes us human. It isn't perfection. As Alexander Pope wrote, "To err is human, to forgive, divine."

Take a moment to reflect on the reading and your response to it.

_____

_____

_____

_____

_____

_____

_____

_____

_____

_____

_____

_____

_____

February 21st

THERE IS A DIFFERENCE BETWEEN crossing someone's boundaries and alerting someone when we see something that does not directly affect us that we believe needs correcting. The way we come to understand the difference is by noticing when this happens.

When our egos are too small, we feel less than, disconnected from the whole. When our egos are too big, we can't actively listen, or balance, because we believe we are the whole. This is missing the mark. From this perspective, we believe we know how others ought to be acting to bring peace to the whole.

We know someone is imposing upon us when they begin a sentence with, "You should." And may I be bold? "Shoulding" on someone is like shitting on them. It's wrong.

How do we know the difference, in the moment? By pausing long enough to determine what we're feeling, and then giving the emotion the space to support us toward the best course of action. In this way, we see what belongs to us and what belongs to them.

On a deeper level, we are all connected. We see clearly that the solution to any given problem is between us and the space – not between us and them. We can ask for help, act appropriately, and then practice letting go of the outcome. We look in the mirror and decide to work only on us.

Feel free to add to this list of instances where boundaries could be set and the instances where shoulding exists. Setting a boundary means speaking up for yourself.

Set a Boundary	Shoulding
Someone bolts in front of you in the meal line.	You shouldn't be writing these messages.
Someone takes your personal property.	You should be drinking more water.
Someone threatens to assault you.	You should clean the table better.
Someone yells in your ear.	You should go on a diet.
Someone "shoulds" on you.	You should do as I say.

The wisdom I'm working on is: when do I set a boundary with someone else, and when do I let go and let God take over? The key, for me, is to become humble, to look at my own actions, and become aware of what emotion I'm working with and any possible character defect that needs my attention and removal.

When someone says, "You should do this," I can take the high road. I have practiced detaching from people who speak to me like this. All the while, I keep faith and hope alive by asking the wisdom mind to bestow blessings upon him, focusing on compassion and tender loving-kindness.

If he's not respecting my boundary of keeping his distance from me, I just breathe and wait for the storm cloud to dissipate. Detachment with love is a sure-fire way to practice the process of meditation for everyone concerned.

How can you detach from someone or something today?

February 22nd

THROUGH OUR PRACTICE, WE CREATE balance in our life. Our focus on ourselves is producing new behavior and a new way of life, one small step at a time. We do this by practicing being awake to all that we can be.

We can imagine these newly defined parts of ourselves: the physical, the mental, the emotional, and the spiritual. We can sit for a while and choose NOW goals for ourselves. But we also have to let go of ego. Once we see clearly what we wish to become, we can let go and take steps in any new direction to decide what fits with our new vision.

As we nourish this moment, we come to feel a sense of self-love that fills the holes where loss has left its mark. We don't achieve anything through willpower. All we have to do is open our awareness and put one foot in front of the other. The creation force within will guide us as we begin to experience the fulfillment of love.

Today, it dawns on me that I practice meditation to see my being. I want to know who I really am! This sacredness fills me up and overflows to others. I am learning to give unconditionally, regardless of any response.

I am becoming more alive than ever before. I am casting off the idea that I am a mistake. I make mistakes and am learning from them.

I have the power to overcome. I write to capture the process. I meditate to move forward into my destiny. It is a valuable usage of time. All I need is my faith!

What, or who, do you have faith in today?

_____

_____

_____

_____

_____

_____

_____

_____

_____

_____

_____

_____

February 23rd

WHAT IF WE CHANGE THE focus when it comes to emotional expression and experience? When we see something we like or dislike, our mind develops a memory of such. The past has the effect of setting up a reaction that is similar to what we have already encountered.

In the present moment, we start at ground zero, observing the feeling state that arises within us, focusing away from the object causing the emotion, and moving towards observing the emotion itself.

Instead of following the thoughts that feed the feeling, we can practice a pattern of observing the emotion as the target. Then we can make a decision to turn our willingness toward examining the intensity and texture of passions that arise within us. In doing so, we own the emotion 100%.

Developing the discipline to focus on the emotional state that emanates from within, the space we give it allows for new patterns of behavior to develop. We come to sense our own solidity because, as every moment passes, that moment dissolves all by itself. The intensity of any emotion changes over time. We come to understand the relativity of that feeling based on the thoughts we feed it in that moment.

What emotions are you giving space to today?

_____

_____

_____

_____

_____

_____

_____

_____

_____

_____

_____

_____

_____

_____

February 24th

Where in the world can you find a forest without a dead tree? The answer is nowhere. A decaying tree provides shelter for creatures; it nourishes the rest of the living trees as it decays into the forest floor.

We can take a lesson from this. Human error is fertilizer for increased intimacy. What we see as a problem is really a chance to be honest about our own shortcomings. In this way, we let our guard down, and others are invited to do so, too. We then develop a closer bond with those we love and those who love us.

Our mistake may be our predestination for future successes. People who cannot see this have not yet learned the lesson of forgiveness. We can learn to forgive ourselves, first by taking responsibility for our actions, learning what we can, and making amends to those involved. We humbly pick up the pieces and plant them in the new garden of our souls. We do this so we can be open to receive love again.

Perfection does not exist. Perfectionism is a spiritual disease. We learn more from our mistakes than we do our successes. We can tell ourselves it's okay to make an error. Then, we can forgive our failures and store our successes.

Imperfection is part of the Universal design, but we don't dwell on it once we have memorized the lesson.

I am not perfect. No one is. One of my tendencies is to take on other people's pain. Once I see this clearly, I can admit it to others, which may invite them to admit their own self-defeating behavior. We can practice letting forgiveness, compassion, and kindness pass through us, then on to others.

What are some self-defeating behaviors of yours?

_____

_____

_____

_____

_____

_____

_____

_____

_____

_____

_____

_____

February 25th

THE ENERGY OF SPITE IS like a suicide bomber. Spite is handing out judgment to get even. That never works, because spite explodes on the one who delivers it as well as the one who receives it.

How do we deal with spite? If we sit with the hurt and breathe out kindness and compassion, there is no fuel to spread the fire of anger. This hurt will pass, just like the tide around the phases of the moon.

When someone hurts us, it's normal to want to get even. But if we give in to spite, we fall into the enemy's trap of being the victim. What if we choose to rise above our opponent, and take a higher view? Can we allow the energy of the harm done to us to touch our hearts? If we can, this will bring us to a place of sadness that only God can heal.

The route the ego takes is toward spite, for it only seeks to protect us. In seeking revenge, the tide of hurt rises and crashes, destroying everything in its path. Spite is a weapon of mass destruction. It affects all of us eventually. Regret usually follows.

If we give the pain a focused point in time and drop it there, we can ask The Universe for help. Then we can practice letting go, while giving The Universe a chance to answer us. This process takes time and patience, encouraging us to see our way forward. This is the path of the spiritual warrior.

How do we practice this in life? The next time someone offends you or hurts you, try to step back. Detach from the person and the experience. Just look at the hurt you feel without of blaming either him or yourself.

When I get hurt, my compulsive thoughts that arise are fierce, but I continue to just be aware of them, giving my anguish as much space as I can muster in the present moment.

There is no winner or loser in this expanded space within. What I experience is an absence of spiteful action on my part, while I move from loneliness to solitude. Being lonely means feeling alone. Being in solitude means being comfortable with who I am and being comfortable on my own. Through the courage I have gained in my spiritual practice, I do not have to lose or feel alone.

What can you do right now to feel less alone?

_____

_____

_____

_____

_____

_____

_____

_____

February 26th

HOW MANY TIMES HAVE WE heard the phrase, "Patience is a virtue"? How do we practice patience? How is the experience comprehended? Staying still and allowing thoughts and feelings to arise, without reaction, allows for first-hand exposure to patience.

Part of practicing patience involves giving up the need to control others. When we believe and act as if we know what is best for our neighbor, we manipulate and control others as targets for our own happiness.

The miracle of the outcome of practicing patience is our awareness of the ego's desire to dominate what thoughts and feelings arise. Giving what emanates from our minds the space to just be, we can lighten up.

Meditation teaches us to let go and let our God or higher power take care of the rest. This takes patience.

How can patience help you in your meditation and in your life?

February 27th

TREAT OTHERS AS WE WISH to be treated. Compassion is putting on someone else's shoes and seeing life through their eyes before we make a decision to act.

When we meditate, we look at ourselves. Don't we secretly wish others would overlook our faults, forgive us, and have compassion for us as human beings?

Forgiveness starts with ourselves and then flows to others. As a stream feeds a river that, in turn, feeds our bays, soon our compassion and forgiveness will swell to the seas and oceans that ebb and flow with greater peace and ease.

Our attitude can change when we forgive ourselves, but we have to believe in the larger picture. This takes faith. Start by trusting in the wisdom inside you.

In our own neighborhoods, we tend to hang around only "our kind." There may be criticism launched at other groups or particular persons. Instead of launching my disapproval right back at the finger pointers, I make a decision not to use any outward judgment. It's an opportunity to inventory my tendency to perpetrate the same negative behavior.

- When do I say someone is "full of sh*t"?

- How often do I consider someone lazy?

- When do I pull the race card?

- How often do I put someone down to build myself up?

- When do I push my own opinion in my need to be right?

- When do I further gossip?

- Do I defame someone else's character?

- Who do I consider to be less than?

- Who do I consider to have worse behaviors than mine?

- Where is my focus when I hear criticism – on them? Or am I compassionate?

- Who or what do I blame for my unhappiness?

I begin to understand that in order to be forgiven for all my wrongs, I must develop the compassion to forgive. The reality is, my actions hurt other people too, sometimes unintentionally. I am really no different from anyone else. Centering myself with a single breath seems to be the key. It starts with a single pause.

When I meditate, I can see all the clouds of negativity and judgment hiding the sun of forgiveness and the sky of compassion. The winter of my discontent with others, turned inward, becomes the Spring of the rebirth of a kind, loving human being.

I'm only hurting myself when I criticize those around me. It is a natural tendency, when I am in my egoic mind with my narrow focus. Being aware of this tendency is the beginning of change. Forgiveness showers down upon my heart, so that it may flow to others and create unity.

What can you forgive in yourself and others today?

February 28th

WHAT ANNOYS US? CAN WE take just a moment to look at pain with a wider view? Our spiritual muscles may be sore from the impact of the exercises in this book. But just being aware and owning our emotions completes the training. Feed the soul and the ache heals faster. We come to believe that all answers arrive from within us.

When we go to the gym, we wait a day or two to let our sore muscles heal and rebuild before we begin again on that specific part of our body. An annoyance works our spiritual muscles. If we continue to feed our aggravation with our thoughts and opinions, the soreness grows.

What if we pause long enough to let the emotion sit within us and let our spirit heal the ache? This is a different kind of exercise program, one that strengthens and increases our stamina for tolerance of other people's flaws. The space we create shows us we all have something that ticks off somebody else.

Happiness does not have to depend on others. We can choose to pass over a small flaw that will disappear from our memories in ten minutes. When we develop tolerance for others, we become gentler as we look inside ourselves.

I'm still new at practicing compassion and patience and creating that space reflexively in the moment. When someone gets in my face with a comment that pushes my buttons, I'm aware that my body constricts and my heart starts to pound. My knee-jerk retort is not always filled with unconditional tender loving-kindness.

Boundary setting, for me, helps me to tolerate another man's insults while creating peace in an unbalanced relationship. Overcoming self-doubt is number one on my list of character flaws, and becoming more conscious of this defect is progress in itself.

After a confrontation, communicating forgiveness is important to me, even if the opposition has a closed heart and ears. I go out for a walk and, replacing the past incident with the present moment, I congratulate myself for exercising my body while dropping every compulsive thought that enters my mind.

I choose to recite a list of what I have for which I am grateful. I can't change that I'm drawn to control negativity, but at least I'm aware of my body's reaction, my compulsive thoughts, and how they feed my feelings of self-doubt.

Taking a breath and starting over with this gratitude list, I blurt out the following statement, "I'm grateful for my willingness to change." A small surge of compassion fills my heart and I sense an instance of healing. I pass that gift to my opponent. I continue to practice letting go and letting God.

Have you identified your biggest character flaw?

February 29th (Leap Year)

DURING MEDITATION PRACTICE, WE ARE becoming more comfortable with watching ourselves. We see our ego. We don't judge it. We just observe and go back to the breath in the present moment of who we are.

This is a still, calm, wise place. We don't think our way to this place. We just are, when we shift to this vast space within.

Everything is invited here. This is the consciousness of pure acceptance and serenity. We cannot capture it. It escapes any measure of control. Instead, we come to know peace as we surrender.

What is your experience of surrender like?

_____

_____

_____

_____

March 1st

Sʜ.ᴛ/ɢ.ᴅ ᴅ.ᴍ./ᴍ. ᴛʜ ꜰ..ᴋ.ʜ ʙ.ᴛᴄ. Words themselves are not good or bad. Perhaps the question is: what emotion do these words help us feed? If we remove the words as speech or thought and sit quietly with the feeling, we become more awake. We begin to resolve the energy from within.

We have learned to react to the words we have grown up hearing. These phrases become part of the recipe for the same meal our ego will digest over and over. It never complains, because it is our familiar coping mechanism.

With meditation, we can start fresh. Every moment can become an unlimited banquet, as we watch ourselves create new recipes with old leftovers. We can suddenly see new words to express the space between passion and aggression, fame and disgrace, praise and blame, and pain and pleasure.

Using old, worn-out words to express negative emotions does not make us any happier. There is so much more to chew on that is healthier and inventive. What will we eat today?

Being less prone to use the repeated phrases that I hear over and over, my main undertaking is to be more compassionate toward those stuck in the revolving door of profanity usage. It's much easier to judge and blame people for their ignorance than to look beneath the surface to address the painful experiences we all share.

It seems clear to me that someone addicted to profanity is just as worthy of compassion. The solution seems to be in creating space between the two factions, with both parties focusing on the more peaceful horizon of balance.

Neither the users of profanity nor the ones who don't, attempt to change the person in front of them. Acceptance and a mirror are the tools for greater tender loving-kindness.

What is your experience of listening to or speaking profanity?

_____

_____

_____

_____

_____

_____

_____

_____

March 2nd

WE CAN FACE OUR PROBLEMS with fear and anger, or with loving-kindness and compassion. An opinion of any given situation is not owned by anyone other than the one who delivers it. Rather than jumping to a fast conclusion based on what we think, we can become still. Then, a peaceful resolve will come.

There's nothing wrong with feeling anything. Bad circumstances can be changed into a situation where honesty creates a bond between two people. It is an opportunity to become more aware of who we are.

Spending time with our feelings, practicing total ownership, and then communicating from a place of compassion, we begin to open up to the truth about reality.

Our egos have opinions. They constrict us. If the focus is on our spirit, there are no losers because we are all one in the spirit. Loving kindness gently touches something painful and allows it to bear its fruit.

Practicing the actions of kindness and compassion brings us new wisdom, but we can't just think it. We learn by doing. We act through faith, keeping an eye on those who have come before us.

Saying "no" for my own self-esteem is the hardest action for me to practice. Pleasing people has been self-defeating. Self-doubt can destroy my life.

Someone asks me to pick up something he needs. He can easily get this himself, but he wants me to do it for him. Pushing my focus away from his wish to avoid personal responsibility, my heart still leads me to say no, because I do not wish to enable him.

I reflexively wish to fix other people's desires, so they'll think more highly of me. When I say no to someone, they might get angry. But this is my decision to make. I base it on the quiet stillness of looking at self-doubt and fear of disapproval directly and allowing that energy to swell up inside me.

How easy is it for you to say "no"?

_____

_____

_____

_____

_____

_____

_____

_____

March 3rd

Spirituality can have humor. Life is filled with negativity; however, constant focus on the prophecy of doom leads to a life out of balance. We can learn to look for humor to uplift ourselves and others. We can begin looking at the larger picture to disarm a pessimistic focus.

Entertainment can have an unexpected twist, not just for us, but for others as well. There are those with whom we can be humorous, and others not. One morning, while I was sitting on my chair, focused on an exercise of meditation, I heard someone outside singing "Jingle Bells." It's March and Spring is around the corner. Hearing the music brought me a sense of joy that I shared with the expanded world around me.

Has anything humorous happened to you lately?

_____

_____

_____

March 4th

SOMEONE ONCE SAID, "WE HAVE two ears and one mouth. Perhaps it is because we can practice listening twice as much as we speak." Opening up to hear someone else's pain doesn't mean we own it. It still belongs to them. By listening, a deeper connection forms.

We all exhibit positive and negative attributes. By practicing listening, there is an opportunity to see how we will react to what another person says or does. Silence, while listening, keeps the focus on our side of the street. We can achieve a more peaceful balance for everyone concerned.

I'm on the road to wisdom when I listen and can accept someone who pushes my buttons of resentment and judgment. People who pass judgment and try to control another's behavior need my compassion. I've been there and done that. I just breathe in the darkness and breathe out the joy and balance of being. By listening to others, I'm actually listening to myself and celebrating our connection to the whole.

Are you making progress in listening to yourself and others?

March 5th

WHEN YOU LOOK AT SOMEONE, do you see their faults or do you see who they are? Our egos seek to evaluate what other people do. Our spirit only seeks to see who people are. Once we see who we are, we become connected to the whole.

It's not hard to find fault with other people. But if we concentrate only on those flaws, we will never get to see the good that we all do. The wisdom is balance. All of us do good and bad things each and every day.

Here is a spiritual truth and a note of caution. If we see only the wrong in others, guess what? We secretly see only the bad in ourselves. Let's all meet in the center of calm and peace. This is the real joy of living.

I avoid people who constantly take inventory of other people's faults. It's not to punish them, but to detach with love. I would rather pray for those people from a distance, allowing them the freedom to be who they are today.

Concentrating on the mirror rather than getting involved in chang-ing others, I am making sure I'm not criticizing them or myself too harshly. With detachment, the space not only gives me the ability to observe myself more objectively, but the insight I receive through the experience helps me skillfully practice the wisdom that is given to me. Applying wisdom into a new way of being shifts the gravity of who I am.

By continuing to take personal inventory, making a list of my assets and defects of character, I can see past my opinions and discern that who I am connects to the entirety of humanity. Living based on my judgments of my emotions relies on something that is foolish – impermanence.

Make a list of your assets and the things you are working on. We all have both!

_____

_____

_____

_____

_____

_____

_____

_____

_____

_____

March 6th

An unobserved emotion is like cooking a meal and then leaving the house with everything on the stove and in the oven. One day, the feast catches fire and burns down the house. A great dinner is tended to with great care and seasoning. Discernment helps us choose the best course of action for the whole. Emotion is best served with wisdom.

What are some observations you have made about emotions?

_____

_____

_____

_____

_____

_____

March 7th

WHEN WE BLAME OUR TROUBLES on someone else or ourselves, everyone loses. There is another option, but it is not for the weak. Drop the blame and invite the pain in for a visit. Sit and look at it and learn the wisdom from it. Put the knowledge in your pocket and drop the pain in the vast empty space we create when we meditate. Some call this God. She will take our pain away when she sees fit. This is emotional success.

When things go wrong, I tend to blame myself. So I sit in meditation to remove the blame. Then, it comes to me. If I identify with the error and make it who I am, it hurts. This is a reaction, something I reflexively do. The higher wisdom is to understand that who I am is still the same. What I do is not who I am. If I forgive the situation, the pain dissolves and I go back to the rest of my evening. And I do.

What is your experience with blame?

_____

_____

March 8th

HAPPINESS DOES NOT HAVE TO depend on others or events. Happiness is grown by opening up our view and dropping opinions of what we think regarding things that have happened. When all else fails, humor is a supply of water that douses the fire of dissatisfaction.

Everyone complains sometimes. Happiness does not come from resolving a complaint; it comes from opening my view and dropping my opinion. Tomorrow there will be a complaint about something else that will be forgotten in twenty-four hours. Look for the humor in life, not the complaints.

When was the last time you cleaned up your attitude toward life? The answer, for me, is NOW!

_____

_____

_____

_____

March 9th

THE WISE, WONDERFUL HEROES INSIDE each of us are waiting to come out now. Don't wait for yours to surface. The Universal Divine Mother cares for and loves who we are. We must open our hearts to the compassion that rightly belongs to us.

Who is your inner hero?

_____

_____

_____

_____

_____

_____

March 10th

WHEN WE RESENT SOMETHING OR someone, we try to resolve the feeling with our egos – typically, over and over. An emotion cannot be resolved. It is energy. When we repent something we have done wrong, we rethink the situation so we can place it in the space of true perspective. Then, we let it go where The Universe dissolves it. All we have to do is be aware and ask for help.

Ultimately, the Supreme Being is in charge of both our spiritual path and the destination. I have an opportunity to look into what is, but not to think of my opinion as a solution. Instead, I sit with an open mind and heart and wait for my intuition to arise. I know that what I think changes from moment to moment. Who I am is eternal.

What is the difference between what you think and who you are?

_____

_____

_____

March 11th

THE MIND HAS THE CAPABILITY to use a fear of past experiences to destroy the consciousness of the present moment. When this happens, we can choose to look at our present fear as an acronym for False Evidence Appearing Real. This is a prime moment to separate who we are from what we think. Wisdom has no form. It expands and surrounds thoughts with a cool calmness that creates peace without force.

I may have my fears, though often unfounded, while being face-to-face with gentleness. My ego is thankful when it has listened to wisdom.

Reminding myself to brave the voice of the past, along with a vow to view the present moment with a fresh approach, I experience a new common-sense insight: Am I appreciating myself, regardless of where I rest?

What do you fear, and what do appreciate about yourself?

_____

_____

March 12th

WISDOM IS VERY MUCH LIKE the phases of the moon or the chirping of a bird. These sights and sounds are always there, but we have to have our eyes and ears open to receive them. Do we know where the moon is in the sky? How do the birds sing? The key is to widen our focus beyond what we do and concentrate on who we are. Are we awake? The Universe is calling us: "Be still and know that I am God…Allah…Dios…Yahweh."

When a storm comes, I can take some time to look at the bad weather. If I believe I am a plastic bag, the storm throws me everywhere it wishes. But if I am the sky, I only have to wait for the storm to pass. I simply ask myself, "Am I a plastic bag or the sky?" It depends on my view.

Today, I am the sky. The storm will pass. Blue sky and the sun will color my life with serenity. I no longer believe I am a plastic bag. That is self-hatred in the worst view of victimhood. Real perspective takes quiet reflection. I'm grateful to find it when I sit.

Sitting with a painful emotion and observing without reacting takes pulling out the space of meditation to real-world situations.

Pausing gives me the perspective of the sky, while reacting makes me the plastic bag.

How can you bring your meditation skills into your daily challenges?

_____

_____

_____

_____

_____

_____

_____

_____

_____

_____

_____

_____

March 13th

LIVING IN THE PRESENT MOMENT rather than focusing on what has happened in the past, or what we cannot know will happen in the future, allows our lives to be enhanced by the wisdom of our spirit. We can then resist the strong pull of emotions and the thoughts of our egos.

Sitting in solitude allows the definitive answer to surface, as we give ourselves the chance to ask the right questions. Allowing time to address our ego's concern, with a focus on the spirit in the "now" helps us to make the best decisions.

I have come to understand that time alone gives me the peace of mind I need to work on myself without any interference. I just keep practicing what I've been reading. Here is what my spirit tells me from the space:

- When you feel like it is necessary, go back, reread, start fresh.

- You have total quiet in which to write.

- You are totally safe from harm. No one can touch you.

- You have enough food.

- You have time to study and practice what you read in solitude.

- You have books that will help you grow.

- You have the opportunity to access the space where unconditional love is unlimited. Every moment is a moment to be with yourself and take in that love.

- Wherever you are in the physical world, there will be imperfections. Your ego will not like this. That's why it's important to practice putting the ego behind the spirit, so that what is real can show itself.

- All difficulty shall pass. It's not permanent. Fighting against it only hurts you – no one else.

- You have what you need today. Open yourself to the compassion, kindness, and love that exist in just being who you are.

Above all, don't take action by another personally. Regardless of what happens to me in this physical world, as a human being, I deserve love. I may not always receive unconditional love from others, but it is plentiful in the cornucopia of God's tender spirit.

Do you believe that you have what you need today? If not, can you sit with that uncertainty? How can you take care of yourself today?

_____

_____

_____

_____

_____

_____

_____

March 14th

WILLINGNESS IS AN ADMIRABLE TRAIT. It is the energy that fuels our hopes, our dreams, and our goals. Willfulness can oftentimes be the force that stalls everything. We lose control of that happy-go-lucky feeling we once had, and we lose interest in everything. Even more, we lose our faith.

It takes tremendous courage to practice willingness when we lose hope and despair. At this moment we must be clear-seeing and gentle with ourselves. Giving up and hiding in our old habits may seem comforting, but that is not clarity or compassion in action. In the Universal view, it is self-hatred at its best. Letting go of perfectionism allows us to make some progress with faith in mind. The rest will take care of itself.

I decide to sit for a moment and meditate on my willingness. I ask the wisdom mind for help. I have two goals to accomplish and not a drop of clarity about either.

Letting go of the chatter in my mind, I arise to take life one very small moment at a time. Acceptance is the answer to all my prayers. Everything else is impermanent.

What are you now willing to do to keep up your meditation practice?

_____

_____

_____

_____

_____

_____

_____

_____

_____

_____

_____

_____

_____

March 15th

IF WE SEE A PERSON for what they say, what they do, or what they look like, we miss who they are. Who we are is only covered up by the physical if we are not awake. All of us are connected by who we are. We are all human beings, not human doings. We must know who we are to turn on the light.

Connecting to who we are as a primary target means moving our personalities to the background while deriving our self-esteem from the vast, empty, magnanimous space of spiritual fulfillment that takes a behavior of stillness to emancipate.

Each moment I draw another breath is a new moment. This point in time is temporary. I make the decision to move to the next instant without holding onto any previous discontent. By letting go, I can see the joy in the next meal or the color of the sky outside my window. I am already connected. I only fool myself if I allow any adverse event to narrow my focus of being human. I rise above through forgiveness, clearing the canvas to paint the next moment.

Can you see a person for who they are, not what they do?

March 16th

SILENT MEDITATION IMPROVES LOVING ENLIGHTENMENT = SMILE.

All answers to life are found within ourselves. Any pain can be overcome by consciously moving the "am" part of "I Am" to the foreground, and then allowing that part to expand until it surrounds the part that hurts. Bathing it with tender loving-kindness and compassion allows for the condition of being human. This is the key to our becoming fully functional, spiritual adults.

When we detach from our egos and sit quietly with our true spirits, our view of life becomes wider and higher. We still have the same feelings as before, but our support system grows larger.

Imagine being a Central American adult who is experiencing his first snowfall. He has never been in a snow-related auto accident, seen a power outage due to snow-laden trees, or felt the icy pain of a snowball hitting his face. All he sees is the wonder of it all – that is the view of the spirit.

Sitting alone in quiet meditation allows us to feed our spirit's focus of the world. This takes work, but we can find a lot more time to give such a project when we just slow down. The question is: "Is it worth it?" We'll never know until we try. What do we have to lose?

There are so many things going on in our lives, other than what is wrong. Negativity is the spotlight of the ego. Our sights get lower and narrower until we usually explode, because the pain is all we can see. Life needs contrast, just as day needs night and happy needs sad. Enlightenment is reaching the middle road where we find peace.

Now, here's the catch. We have to learn to become our own best friend. The spiritual part of us knows how. Notice I did not say the religious part. Religion is something we practice – we do. Our spirits are waiting to be uncovered. We only need to sit, awakening, merely being ourselves.

If we're having trouble "being," we ask someone to help who knows how to accomplish this task. They're the ones with the kindness, compassion, peace, and balance in many of the things they do. Just don't forget the human part. That makes us imperfect. As we forgive ourselves, we begin to experience forgiveness for everyone because, after all, we are all spiritually connected to the whole Universe.

Can you identify "I" as the ego, thinking mind, and "AM" as my awareness that I am human? How are your thoughts and your inner awareness of yourself different now?

_____

_____

_____

_____

_____

_____

March 17th

JUST BE. I KNOW I keep talking about living in the present moment. Well, what does that mean? Those of us writing and talking about this share the benefits of learning from the past and the importance of letting those former moments pass. Being totally present means being emotionally, thoughtfully, physically, spiritually, and volitionally sentient, aware.

We cannot be fully present if we hold onto the past. We miss all the present wonder, the ability to sit with what is happening right now. At the end of each day, we can mentally wash the chalk inscriptions from the board of life and start again. Sometimes, during a particularly hectic day, that means taking in a new breath and starting over at the exhale. Our souls only know now; they don't experience time.

If we are trying, in our minds, to relive the past to correct a mistake, or if we are worried about the future, we miss the serendipity of the day. We overlook the chance to feel the warmth of the sun, to appreciate the simple joy of drinking a cold cup of water, or to experience gratitude after having a full meal. We might never get what we want today, but we can certainly widen our perspective to see what we have to be thankful for.

Jesus Christ was recorded as saying, "I and the Father are one." I look at Christ's statement and take it into meditation. I am surprised as to what I find true today. If each present moment of now is the only important moment, and if I make the decision to put the spirit of a higher power in front and the ego of my desires in the background, then I, too, can see the sagacity of Jesus' words.

My spirit is connected to the Universe of God, as it is intended, observing the natural rhythm of existence. Now, I may not be able to operate 24/7 on this new revelation, but all I have to deal with is the moment of now. If I start compulsively ruminating, I just say, "thinking," and go back to my breath.

This spiritual path has so many more options to choose from. All I have to do is be open enough to receive them. Then, I can make a decision that leads to peace of mind – for me and the world at large. The urge to be right falls away as a cause of frustration.

As Christians say, I can be reborn, just by making the choice to put my spirit in front of my ego. It's as simple as taking a breath in meditation. And just for the moment, I grasp the experience of the creator and myself as one.

What is your experience with starting over, at any given moment?

_____

_____

_____

_____

_____

March 18th

TODAY IS A DAY TO practice being kind to ourselves. Our idea of living from wanting-to-wanting leads to more wanting. The idea of "having" leads to more having. Sometimes, if we're aware, we can realize we have so many thoughts running around in our heads and many of them are not helping us to be kind to ourselves.

The first step is to sit quietly in meditation, becoming aware of individual thoughts. Once we do that, we can see several things. The first thing we can see is how many thoughts seem to be strung out on the line, like a mix of fresh and dirty laundry. The next thing we can see is that we do not have to change a thing about this – we can just sit and watch. After a while, we may see all of the thoughts labeled either good or bad. Here is where we can make a change. What if we didn't label them at all? What if we accepted them as thoughts pertaining only to our physical existence?

Have you ever seen someone sitting with one leg and foot jiggling up and down? Maybe we would label them as troubled, fearful, angry, or simply possessing a lot of nervous energy. This is compulsive thinking. The foot jiggling doesn't have to be labeled at all. Perhaps the best thing we can do is notice that it's happening. Then, we can stop, center ourselves, and sit quietly with the feelings that arise. Just like we would notice this jiggling of thoughts, the goal is not to stop the thoughts, but to accept that they're coming – one after the other. Then, without labeling them, the silent breath we add to the mix gently stops the train without any effort.

Our goal is not to have an empty mind. Our awareness of the thoughts, dropping them in a space of loving kindness, becomes the gentle ambition. The moments of silence and peace that result, however few in the beginning of practice, will take care of themselves. This is the start of being kinder to ourselves.

On some days this door will open wider than on other days. Again, just being aware is the goal, not how wide the door opens. When thinking takes the place of being, then that's the place of "dis-ease". Focusing on being takes work and we have the rest of our lives to practice.

Once we become conscious of our thoughts and we practice letting them go, we experience an instant of peace that can grow. This is the seed to germinate in the garden of tender loving-kindness.

Today I am not feeling well. Accepting this reflection, but not buying into it, severs the cord of my biggest character defect – self-doubt. Allowing myself to experience silence, with feelings in tow, I can ask for help from others around me. I make myself a cup of hot tea to soothe myself.

What do you do when you're not feeling well?

_____

_____

_____

March 19th

LABELS, LABELS, LABELS! IT IS a lie that we become the color of our skin, a fatality from our childhood, our educational background, or even the language we speak daily. Society does not teach us this, but there is something deeper within us that can show us the process towards wisdom. The problem is, if we continue doing more and more, we never get to sit quietly long enough to get to the bottom of things – to see who we really are.

But we all have something in common. We can all look in the mirror and see the inventory of all we do, covering who we are beneath our bodies. When we comb our hair, brush our teeth, or wash our face, we may not be aware that not all human beings can see within themselves. It's like the perfectly wrapped Christmas package that some of us never choose to open. It's always under the tree, always fresh, and always a joyful mystery. But we have to look for it there.

Telling ourselves we don't have time to take stock of who we are is folly. We can make the time to look for the gift that is us, but it takes courage. The natural abilities within us may be buried under a mountain of overused words or actions, or hidden by anger, fear, guilt, and shame.

With faith in hand, we go looking for this gift of our being-ness, slowly. And we don't have to do it alone. The more we think we're different from others, the further we move away from the discovery.

Once we get below the components of what we do, what we say, what we think, and what we feel, we come to know that all of us are connected to the endowment of who we are. From the moment we are born until we die, the secret is there to be discovered. All we have to do is be awake and come to know and listen – to be whole.

Besides who we are, when we open the box that says "today," it is even more important that we view the events from the perspective that we simply *are*, rather than focus on reacting to what life's moments bring us. Who we are has limitless possibilities. Here we find the endless love for being human.

Today I accidentally disturbed someone, who reacted with anger. I acknowledge my humanity and also forgive him for his, without discussing anything with him directly. I'm not here to change him, only to accept what is; and when I am wrong, promptly admit it. So I apologized.

He then gave me a very helpful suggestion, so that I could contact him in the future in a way that would not disturb him. That is the gift of today! I can receive help and get my needs met without being defensive in the process. I make a choice to go below the wrapping labels of what we do and address a character flaw that is keeping me from being peaceful.

What is your experience today with letting go of labels?

March 20th

DEVELOPING A SPIRITUAL RELATIONSHIP CAN change how we comprehend time. Rather than spending countless moments ruminating over past events or future prospects, developing the gentle discipline to live in the present moment of now is a practice that actually expands our sense of time.

Being conscious of our bodies, thoughts, emotions, and our interconnected life breaths in a calm, ever-progressing, concentration of focus, leaves little time for the mind to wander.

There is no passage of time in the spirit. Pure consciousness just is. What we encounter as sentient beings becomes bent and distorted by our ego-centered senses.

After lunch, sitting quietly on my bed, I realize that time can be treated like a meal. As I open my mouth to receive the meal, I think, what if I refuse to eat this meal? I would be hungry. And if I refuse to meditate, that would be an act of shutting down my soul. Having the choice of attending to life as it comes to me is the real banquet. I've come to realize that prayer is nothing more than a conversation I'm having with the whole creation of The Universe. Meditation is just listening, an openness to awareness, without any expectation.

Spending time alone gives me moments to set my mind to the side, to open my soul to life, kindness, compassion, and the love of peace that only comes from the still, quiet voice inside me.

The Universe really loves me. When I think about the past, it is I who have shut the door. I was taught to do so and the fact that it became a habit is another thought I watch come and go. I know how to open myself by using present-moment consciousness. I have the wisdom to open a portal to love when pain has occurred. I have to continue to make a decision to keep my spiritual senses open to receive the bounty of what life has to offer. Living in the present moment is the key process.

Life's difficult and challenging situations, cultivated in the rich soil of the present moment, will always have meaning and purpose waiting to be discovered. All I need do is add the water of willingness.

Do you have a healthy, balanced relationship with the present moment? What can you do to be more aware of your mind's habits while you meditate? Write your habits and your intention here.

_____

_____

_____

_____

_____

_____

March 21st

WE CAN ACT OUT OF wisdom or we can react to things, people, places, and ideas. If we're not sure about the wisdom of what to do or not do, we can become aware of what we feel. Are we afraid, angry, lonely, ashamed, or even joyful? Once we know what we feel, then the real miracle of understanding starts to emerge. But first, we have to be awake and open to who we are.

Who we are is not what we feel or what we do. Once we accept those facts, the wisdom of who we are, whether alive on this earth, or free from our bodies after death, is timeless and constant. All we have to do is create a habit of sitting quietly with ourselves long enough to understand this vision.

Using this discipline of living in the present moment, we can use the complementary relationship between distinctly separate feeling states and the mindful observer of who we are. We only react when we believe what we feel is permanent. Wisdom teaches us that feelings come and go, just the same as every passing moment.

The only thing constant is our breath. Here is where we become anchored to who we are. This is where we come to accept the passage of time, making better choices in each moment.

Changing the focus from the impermanent, from what we do to who we are, takes courage and daily commitment. What we do from moment to moment now depends on the wider view of how it affects the whole Universe, not one individual over the other. We are all bound to the who-we-are of creation. That's serene wisdom. It is an illusion that we think and feel differently from one another. The only constancy is that everything changes and passes.

We're all in this together, whether we like it or not. When we face what we don't like, there is a chance to journey inside ourselves – to eat the false ego of who we think we are and let it dissolve.

God, grant me the serenity to accept the things I cannot change, the courage to change the things I can, and the wisdom to know the difference.

This is the simplest, most non-religious, prayer I know. The words haven't changed, but I have evolved to embrace it in a new and different way over the years. Today, it is all about listening and watching, creating a sufficient pause to see more clearly how to act on the energy of wisdom.

Do you have a prayer that opens your heart to receive wisdom? Write it here.

_____

_____

_____

_____

_____

March 22nd

WHAT IS PAIN FOR? WE may keep asking ourselves this question. Perhaps we have done so for many years. Why did I have a troubled childhood? The deeper we look at these types of discussions, the darker it gets. The darker it gets, the more complaining we do. The more we complain, the more our attitudes color various moments of our day. While sitting quietly, doing my best to let go of the current self-talk, I come upon a very simple answer in a brief instance of silence.

Maybe, for a while, this answer doesn't make any sense. Then, Bam! The wall of ignorance falls down. This is part of the cycle of life. The Universe wishes to experience life through us in this way. We can stop blaming ourselves and start listening to the simple voice of our spirit. From birth, we have experienced growing pains all the way through the point of adulthood. But our spiritual growth is meant to continue taking us down the path we are supposed to travel.

Just as autumn turns into winter and winter into spring, we can develop a style to watch and befriend ourselves as our lives wane and wax from season to season. We can witness the creation of new buds for growth in times of emotionally cold darkness. We can practice being with ourselves and turning loneliness into solitude. We can become our own best friends.

This is the time to sit and practice self-kindness, real compassion, and inner peace. We make the time to alter our perspective and to stop taking things so personally. By doing so, we develop less of a desire to cling to all the pleasures our personalities yearn for.

We can sit with the discomfort of what we term pain, only to realize it's a natural occurrence of the changing of a season. Leaning into the grief of what is can create new strength.

We can stumble blindly and painfully down the road of life, or we can choose to see a more joyous connection as we open our spirits to a never-ending supply of wisdom. Perfection is not the goal – it's being a part of the whole.

What season of life are you in right now? Is it a cold winter of disappointment and frustration, or a spring of new growth? Maybe it's summertime, and you're more carefree, or it's fall, a time of preparation.

_____

_____

_____

_____

_____

_____

March 23rd

OTHER PEOPLE'S OPINIONS OF ME are none of my business. This is easier to say than it is to practice. We must have faith in grace while expanding our spirit as our primary source of inspiration. Then, we have to "act as if" until creation happens. The more we innovate with The Universe, the more love fills our cup. Consequently, love can run over to others. The Buddhists call this Tonglen. Christians call it charity. It matters not what we call it, but that we become human beings who can avoid grasping substance.

Life brings on a more meaningful purpose for us, as well as those whose path we touch. Other people can never know who we are, but if we know, then we intuitively understand the connection to the whole. Our egos have opinions that can create a constant, compulsive, inner dialogue of negativity that is usually wrong. Learning to place our spiritual part in front of our egos allows us to watch our lives consciously. Through this cutting-edge focus, we develop greater power and truth.

If I worry about what people are saying behind my back, or stress over the dissatisfaction they express to my face, I give them the power to control how I feel, how I see myself, and how I act out the moments, hours, and days of my life. I can either live a soap opera life, with silly commercials, or choose to live a full-length documentary worthy of an Academy Award nomination. It is my choice.

In the morning, before writing, I spend a short time breathing in the source of love from wherever it comes in the Universe, without definition. The importance is to open my heart to the possibility of tender loving-kindness. Then, I exhale the love I receive outward toward other people through a long stream of meditation.

Some people are very close to me, while others are only passing by in my field of peripheral vision. The hardest part of my practice concerns the people my ego insists on calling enemies. I breathe in the pain and send out compassion to them anyway, because those enlightened before me suggested I give it a while and experience it for myself. It is their opinion my ego fears the most. But this is folly.

This practice shows me so much light. First, I soak in as much love as my soul can hold. Yet, I don't hold on to it. I breathe it outward and give it away. When I do this for my supposed enemies, it heals the dark parts within me that push away love. I find these adversaries represent the parts of me that I don't allow love to enter. By forgiving them, I forgive myself. I begin to understand how we are all connected.

After meditating, I look outside my window to see the grass, clover, and dandelions that are starting to sprout in the yard. I see a honey-bee laboring hard over the wildflowers to gather what is needed for a day's work. This is a view from my spirit – not from my short-sighted, selfish ego.

I catch a glimpse of the sun coming out from behind a cloud. My room is bathed in a bright light, and I stop writing to look around the room. This isn't a coincidence. For a moment, the Universe is responding to what I am creating on paper. As I breathe out joy and pick up my pencil, the clouds cover the sun. I sense the cyclical order of things and I feel peaceful. Listening to my soul is more satisfying than anyone else's opinion of me.

What inspires you today?

_____

_____

_____

_____

_____

_____

_____

_____

_____

_____

_____

_____

March 24th

W<small>ITH LARGER EYES, LET US</small> be here with gentleness and compassion towards ourselves. With that expanded outlook, we can see more honestly, without our defenses.

Once we are honest, kind, and compassionate before the whole Universe, we can make the decision to let go and move on to the next moment. We don't slam the door on the past. Neither would we wish to relive those moments over and over, once we have faced the whole truth.

We have learned to lean headlong into the pain we have feared the most. We have invited this torment to sit right beside us without judgment. We have removed every whirling thought that gathers in our minds.

We come to sit, even for an instant, in forgiving silence that comes with living fully in the present moment. This is our practice.

I face today with many thoughts that can mask developing my practice of self-forgiveness. I'm thinking about words people say that are harmful. I ask myself, *"When do I use words that are helpful or hurtful in the long run?"* There are so many directions to go, but I have to widen what I see. The encouragement I seek comes from my faith within. I tend to see it after I do it. Then, I understand it.

The compulsive chatter in my mind is another destructive force. These thoughts defend me, but they also fuel the painful feelings I am trying to solve. Then, I remember feelings aren't solved. They resolve in silence.

I heard about a hiker who came upon a butterfly struggling to escape its cocoon. Wishing to relieve the insect of its apparent pain, he whipped out his pocketknife, and with the greatest intentions of kindness, cut into its cocoon attempting to usher in an early release. But the traveler learned a valuable lesson that day. The act of squeezing out of its spun tomb was nature's way of pushing all the necessary fluids into the butterfly's new wings. Premature removal left the butterfly with crumpled, inoperative limbs. Unable to fly, it walked away clumsily and died within a few hours.

Life has a design. Trying to figure it out creates more madness for me. Trying to control life makes for hell on Earth. Today I'm in my own cocoon, feeling some pain and regret. The solution is never found outside. The question I ask myself is, *"How much time will I spend alone, squeezing out my wings, so when my time is up, I can fly away?*

How can you take care of yourself today as you sit with painful emotions?

_____

_____

_____

_____

_____

March 25th

START TODAY WITH THE IDEA of a cloudless, blue sky that seems to go on forever. Now imagine sitting upon the highest mountain and looking out at the same view. Now sit and watch. Let the clouds roll in one at a time but keep your perspective on the sky. Those clouds and the developing storms are the faults and shortcomings in our lives. It may be hard to look at them. We may feel ourselves suffering, as we attempt to pull away in pain.

Now, remember the sky. Go past it. Go on past the moon, the sun, the solar system, and on to the edge of the galaxy. All of this huge space exists outside of us. The same space exists inside us as well, but we have to go and find it. Perhaps it is the pain we feel that starts this journey outward and inward. Instead of clearly seeing the discomfort, our natural tendency is to push away from the table of now. We don't want this meal in front of us. But, if we sit and open ourselves to the experience, we can start to see that what is painful exists in a larger field, surrounded by love, compassion, and kindness.

A moment from the past: I remember the first time I became over-confident. It was after learning to ride my bicycle. I came crashing down onto the street, tearing up my knees and elbows. My shorts were no protection. I ran home with blood running down my legs and arms. But next, there was a warm bath to wash away the blood and a gentle soap to remove the small, embedded stones and dirt. Afterwards, there was a generous application of stinging Merthiolate to disinfect.

Finally, large gauze pads were applied with first aid tape, gently covering the wounds, creating the environment to heal. Isolating the accepted damage allowed for slow healing, along with protection from any future infection. The exercise became my acceptance of the discomfort of my skinned body, in addition to the experience of a gentle, soothing care complete with compassion and tenderness.

After a few days, the third leg of my process entered my wisdom mind. The pain was no longer there. It wasn't as permanent, as I had originally led myself to believe. I can still draw on this lesson today. I can see how time is fleeting. It has been decades since that moment; however, I realize that this present moment will pass into emptiness as well.

Now that I have this larger perspective, I can see time and space as vivid in the moment. Yet this moment also dies as it is replaced by the next moment and the next. Life is impermanent, but I can draw on kindness and compassion that have no end. I must deal honestly and directly with the reality of life, both the moments of sunshine and of rain. I surround myself with love, charity, and the openness of space and time that can heal.

I make a decision to be the sky.

Are you the cloud or the sky today?

_____

_____

_____

March 26th

"Bang!" Let's begin today with the concept of the beginning of the Universe, the Big Bang theory. First, there was nothing. Then, scientists tell us there was a huge explosion hundreds of billions of years ago. Now, let's go to the moment where something started from nothing. Right there! There's a relationship between the nothingness and the "something-ness." It's fresh, new, untouched by flaw. There are no labels. It is much more basic than even the uniting of sperm and egg. More basic than the start of a human being.

Now, arise with exactly the same freshness. Start with any breath. Be conscious. Breathe in and exhale. For some, that's Genesis. For Christians, it is being born again in the Holy Spirit. For Muslims, it is the time taken to pause in prayer during the day. Buddhists choose sitting in silence to become aware of the "self" beyond the constant chatter of our minds.

Being conscious is faith in action. Life can start over at any chosen breath, leaving behind the previous breath as a dream. Each moment can be a "big bang", but only if we choose to create that idea of being awake with every respiration.

We can start to see an image of our unknowingness. Are we something or nothing? Which one shall we choose? Are we a physical body with a spiritual foundation, or are we a spiritual awareness inside a physical body? Most likely, we find this question unanswerable. Being human is a paradox. We are both spiritual and physical. We are neither and both. Again, the key to serenity, in this relationship, is starting fresh. Starting at the same point that started it all. Recreate that moment and find the peace there.

The practical way of experiencing the "Big Bang" daily is to choose a time to sit still. My aim is to quiet my body and my mouth. Once I've done that, and I breathe, I am faced with the Big Bang of the compulsive conversation in my mind. My goal is not to silence this chatter. That's like trying to stop the explosion of creation. I just observe its happening and go back to the beginning, with the emptiness of starting over with my breath.

If I don't experience a train of monumental silence, I just accept that and start over. The goal is not to hush the clamor, but to be aware and to be with my breath. If I find myself thinking up a storm, I just go back to the moment before the Big Bang and say "thinking." Then, I start over. Each time I begin again, I continue to go back to the point of awareness that parallels the starting of the Universe.

I am not here to master this method. I am only willing to practice it and let go. I do this at least once daily, but sometimes as much as four times. I experience the habit of starting over with a fresh, expanded, less cluttered space than ever before. This path has not been a straight line. My path is different and unique to me.

How is your compulsive mind chatter today?

_____

_____

March 27th

NATIVE AMERICANS SAY, "JUDGE NOT a man until you have walked a mile in his moccasins." This is an important step to free ourselves from the narrowing power of selfish ego. When we search for the viewpoints of others, we begin the process of understanding true compassion. We all have egos. We all fall prey to our own selfishness. No one escapes opinions or feelings.

The compassion we develop by looking at life through another person's eyes can soften our own harsh criticism. We're brought closer to others by empathizing with the pain and the joy we share in common. We all have the same doubts, fears, anger, sadness, and loneliness. Rather than getting bogged down in hiding from all of this perceived darkness, compassion becomes a beacon that we can share outwardly.

Imagine being in a large, darkened field with thousands of people. You are in the pitch of night, under a heavy cloud cover. There is no moon. No stars provide the light of faith, hope, or love. Now put yourself in the hearts and minds of all those around you in that somberness. There is only a hollow breeze and silence. Imagine the fear, the loneliness, and the separateness that each of us feels in zero visibility. Feel the tremendous need of all the people.

Now reach into your pocket and pull out your own candle of compassion. Light it to pierce the darkness. Out of the spiritual component that binds us together, encourage the person next to you to risk allowing you to light their candle. Pass the flame of hope in every possible direction. Now wait and watch. Each person has the choice to reach to the front, back, left, and right - to pass a light that connects. A single flame grows to dozens, growing faster and larger, until the whole field is illuminated with the light of grace.

Soak in all that luminosity. If someone's flame goes out accidentally, someone close by relights their candle and faith is restored.

Now imagine standing in the field, asking everyone to extinguish their flames. The whole field is plunged back into blackness. The awkwardness of fear and disconnection returns. Then, reach into your pocket again. Light your candle. Pass the light along. In a fresh moment, the darkness is driven back by the growing light of passing torches.

When we first learn the wisdom of feeling and expressing compassion, it becomes easier to create hope again – whenever there is a need. Perhaps, this is the mystery of the second coming of Christ. At any moment, when there is a real lack, we use a fresh start, rather than judging one another. We give what we know truthfully. It pierces the darkness of hopelessness and despair. The second coming of compassion can be recreated by being awake, then acting.

Today's topic relates to the idea of seeing ourselves as a victim. Every day we have a choice. Do we spend our days wallowing in our own darkness and hating others who have done us wrong? Or do we open our heart and see that others are suffering, too? I light the flame of compassion for myself first. Then, I deliver it to another. This is not a single occurrence. Over time, there will be many opportunities for a second coming, each following every possible, present moment. I am aware of my breath. I light my flame anew.

Are you dwelling on hate and regret today? Can you see that others are suffering, too? Write about that here.

_____

_____

_____

_____

_____

_____

_____

_____

_____

_____

_____

_____

March 28th

GLENDA THE GOOD WITCH OF the North from the movie "The Wizard of Oz" said, "It's always best if we start at the beginning." This wisdom statement applies to us, as well, every day. When we open up and love ourselves from the perspective of who we are, we experience calm. But when we think about all the things we have said or done we will run into roadblocks. Because the things we have done that we regret have paved the way for suffering – both within ourselves and others.

We can look at Dorothy and her adventures with the Scarecrow, the Tin Man, and the Cowardly Lion. In reality, they are reflections of our own humanity. Dorothy practices grace within the short-comings of all three of the other characters. In helping them, she helps herself because her companions are merely counterparts of her inward self. The pseudo-truth of separateness is an illusion.

The prefix, "co" has a root meaning of togetherness. Passion is the experience of understanding the painful struggle in life. Practicing mercy starts from within and then can be extended to others because we can relate. This is compassion.

Opening up to any pain we experience, whether created or received, is a courageous act. Compassion heals from the soul, without judgment or fault-finding. The soul knows no fault because there is only one soul to which we either choose to connect or not. Sides do not exist in the spiritual realm. All we have to do is breathe inward and start over at any time. If something goes wrong, we can acknowledge it and start over in the present moment.

The more I judge others, the more harshly I lash out at myself. Being conscious acknowledges and loves the whole. It reminds me of a humorous story I once heard:

All the parts of the body got together to discuss what part was supreme. The brain started by touting its superior intellect. Without the brain's direction, nothing would happen. The heart interrupted to proclaim that without its ability to circulate the blood and to feel love for the body, there would be no enjoyment in life. The hands and the legs then fought over which was more valuable. Was it the ability to walk from place to place, or the ability to write, touch, and get things done? The lungs took a deep breath and bellowed that, without them, the body would have no way of creating life's breath.

The more one body part proclaimed its superiority, the more the other parts grew louder. There ensued quite an uproar. Then, the anus opened and started to proclaim its worth. There was a small amount of silence. Then, all the parts of the body began to laugh in unison, calling it smelly and worthless.

The anus became enraged and decided to teach the rest of the body a lesson. It shut down and would let nothing pass. Soon the body began to fill up with waste. The brain became dizzy. The lungs panted heavily, as the heart started skipping beats, the legs faltered, and the arms had no strength to keep the body from falling to the ground. The anus held its turf, until every part surrendered to its importance.

Then, the anus proclaimed, "We all have our function and our service to the flesh. We are all equal. We need to remember we are bound to work together for the greater good." With that, all the body parts sighed with relief to a lesson learned. All returned to a normal function.

We all have good and bad within. We all deserve compassion as a result. We can forgive ourselves. We forgive others, as we wish to be forgiven. This dynamic includes everyone. Even the most evil character has an opportunity to pass commiseration in both directions. We can no longer afford to think of ourselves as alone. Wars are created out of self-righteousness.

I can choose to focus on three simple elements as I carry out my day:

- Be more conscious of who or what I regard with disgust and greed.
- Make a decision to open up to the space where tender loving-kindness comes from within.
- Once filled to the brim, I can elect to pass compassion to anyone I meet, whether they have it in return or not.

Practice these three steps today. Write down your experience here.

_____

_____

_____

_____

_____

_____

March 29th

TODAY WE CAN SPEND SOME time being aware of what attracts us and draws us closer— whether it is a person, place, thing, feeling, or state of mind. Pleasure is something we naturally move toward. We can also spend time being aware of what we avoid. Now, we can go a step further and become familiar with that which we normally ignore. What are we missing while we are absorbed with ourselves?

By looking at what brings us pleasure, pain, and ignorance, we can create an awareness to grow personally. We are learning not to suppress any emotions, nor to act them out in the world and create more suffering for ourselves and The Universe.

Genuine peace comes from accepting exactly what is happening in the moment. We don't have to like it. We can be honest about our feelings without reacting to them. We may struggle a bit to find this acceptance and peace. Nevertheless, we have an opportunity to trust in this wisdom. We only have to sit still with what we feel, until a universal revelation comes to us in its own time.

To reach peace and joy, I must accept myself while being open to learn. I am working on allowing the three categories of pleasure, pain, and ignorance to bring me to a new sense of spiritual maturity. I'm no saint, but I can use my meditation as an opportunity to get closer to who I am and to move away from my ego. I can lean into discomfort and develop the courage to be a warrior of great internal strength.

Finally, right in the middle of what I usually tend to totally ignore, there are seeds of wisdom from which I can draw some strength. Just for the moment, I open my heart to discomfort, while being gentle and affirming to myself without the need to cling to my wants. I must be willing to continue to remain open, expanding my courage to the vast possibilities of which I am unaware today.

In sitting, I breathe in the pain of regret and breathe out the peace of what is not yet realized. I start with myself and then extend to all who may feel this way in the moment. Feeling the connection, when I practice, is a simple service to the whole.

Hindsight is always 20/20. The most important thing I can do is stay present to whatever comes to my consciousness. Whatever happens in a year probably won't be significant. To test this hypothesis, I go back a year and try to remember the details of the whole day. Enough said.

Are you making progress in seeing life's moments as impermanent? Write about your perspective here.

_____

_____

_____

_____

_____

_____

March 30th

SOCIETY SEEMS VERY INTERESTED IN educating everyone. Public school is mandatory. We can ask the question, "Does that really improve us in a way that everyone benefits?" What is not taught in school is real wisdom. We might call that EQ (Emotional Quotient/Intelligence).

Beginning with our own inventory, we must look for this wisdom with clear-sighted honesty. The first fundamental truth to practice is a gentle, kind, compassionate approach to the journey. This is one of the amazing benefits of meditation.

Remember the story of the tortoise and the hare? Slow and steady wins the race. This innate wisdom provides the key to understanding the phrase, "A chain is only as strong as its weakest link."

We can draw on other areas of our lives to improve our EQ. When we go to the gym, a dedicated athlete will tell us, "No pain, no gain." Keeping the idea of a gentle approach in mind, we can bring our focus to the concept of emotional exercise.

There are two ways to exercise our emotional growth. First, there is the sending and receiving of basic emotional states, without the mind becoming "interruptive." Secondly, as soon as we start to evaluate a situation, either positive or negative, and our mind/ego starts to take over, we can make a decision to go straight to the heart. Here we treat pain and pleasure as something to observe, rather than respond reflexively.

Making a commitment to use our breath to guide our emotional growth is wisdom in action. Now we can work with pain and pleasure in our new exercise program, keeping in mind the lessons already learned in the physical gym. As we breathe in what is painful, we sit with the weight of the darkness. Just before breathing out, we open our hearts to the discomfort, and with a wider faith, we breathe out an invitation to a broader solution that will come in its own time to increase our insight.

Today let's practice taking ourselves to a larger view as we breathe. What is troubling you today? Allow your mind to gently focus on that, and then make a choice to drop the thinking process. Visualize others who have similar troubles. It's not my team vs. your team. Just breathe and allow compassion and kindness to drive this moment of healing discernment.

With each breath, we venture out to a larger and larger group, until we are in a relationship with the whole world. Your pain is my pain, and my pain is yours. I can see this moment connecting us. What I wish for myself, I wish for others. The wisdom is that there is no break in the connection perceived by my mind. Our chain is only as strong as its weakest link, and our connection works to strengthen that chain.

What brings me enjoyment can be treated in the same way. When I hear music I love, I breathe in the symphony of gladness. Then, I breathe it out for others to enjoy. My ego may say to hold onto it for myself, but I'm reminded I'm in the emotional gym and training for a marathon. I don't hold onto the joy, as my ego urges. I briefly see and feel the pleasure for what it is, then I start sending it to those I love dearly. With each breath inward and outward, I can increase the scope to my family, friends, everyday people I see in my town, and even to my enemies.

Sending joy out to my enemies is not going to fly right away. I have to "fake it 'til I make it". For me, this is an underdeveloped emotional muscle. I have found wisdom creeps in slowly. Something inside me changes when I wish to give contentment to those that conjure up fear and anger. The darkness within me, where no openness or daylight has pierced for years, begins to unfold to a newfound sense of relief. In loving my enemies, I come to love all of myself. My neighbor and I are all connected in view of this experience. When I am kind to others, being compassionately aware, I am becoming someone I respect. I am becoming my own best friend.

What is your experience with kindness today?

_____

_____

_____

_____

_____

_____

_____

March 31ˢᵗ

WHEN FACED WITH A SITUATION that brings out the worst in us, we can give ourselves time to learn from it, and expand our growth as spiritual human beings. Concepts like this can be used to open our eyes and to wake up. All we have to do is make a decision to be aware and see all that is possible to comprehend. Normally, we just react! Now is the perfect occasion to look at problems with a broader appreciation.

When we do what we have always done, we get what we have always gotten. Change involves acting our way into a new way of being. We need two things to achieve this new action – willingness and a practice period. We cannot run any distance, until we first tie our shoes.

Have you ever been in conversation with someone who won't stop talking and complaining? Maybe they get loud and start insulting you. What is your first reaction? Annoyance, anger? Me, too. What are your options? Well, you could yell back, shove the guy, or worse. And where does that get you? Fights can end badly, as we all know. We know another way.

I've learned it's just not worth it to get into a fight with someone who is in a dark place. I don't want to go there anymore, so I pull back quietly. From a safe distance, several points of discernment come to light:

- Eventually, this unhappy talker will tire and stop. He cannot go on forever. This is like a thunderstorm that will eventually pass.
- This is an opportunity for me to see his pain and increase my ability to grow in patience and understanding. The larger view is coming.

Practice removing yourself from an angry encounter. Write about that experience here.

_____

_____

_____

_____

_____

_____

_____

_____

_____

_____

SERIES INFORMATION

Thank you so much for completing *Beginning, A Human's Guide to Inner Compassion*, which is Book One in a Four-Book Series. To continue your experience, please access the next three books in the series!

All Four Books In The Series

Book One: *Beginning, A Human's Guide to Inner Compassion*
January 1st through March 31st

Book Two: *Maintain, A Human's Guide to Inner Compassion*
April 1st through June 30th

Book Three: *Fade, A Human's Guide to Inner Compassion*
July 1st through September 30th

Book Four: *Wilderness, A Human's Guide to Inner Compassion*
October 1st through December 31st

About the Author

CRAIG BYRNES IS A TEACHER, author, and the CEO of Our Mindful Process, an educational group that teaches mindfulness meditation, which involves learning how to conquer old life patterns, practice forgiveness, and move forward to a place of self-validation.

"We teach people why being curious about who we are, not what we think, elevates us, frees us and empowers us!"

Craig's extensive research and experience with mindfulness meditation inform this book series and his work. With the readings and guided meditations in this book, Craig's intention is to teach us how to live peacefully in an increasingly difficult and violent world. The techniques and insights in this series are directly applicable to daily life.

Craig is well known in the gay community as the creator of the International Bear Brotherhood Flag, which is a pride flag that represents the beloved bear subculture within the LGBTQIA community.

He lives in Washington, D.C.